Chimichurri

A Chimichurri Cookbook with Delicious Chimichurri Recipes

By
BookSumo Press

Published by
http://www.booksumo.com

LEGAL NOTES

Table of Contents

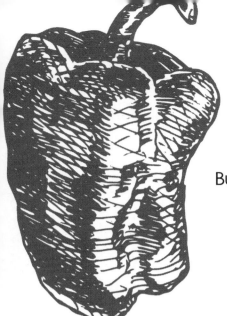

How to Make
a Full Chimichurri

🥣 Prep Time: 1 h
🕐 Total Time: 1 h

Servings per Recipe: 10
Calories   55.5
Fat   5.5g
Cholesterol   0.0mg
Sodium   236.2mg
Carbohydrates   1.4g
Protein   0.3g

Ingredients

2 garlic cloves, minced
1 tsp coarse salt
1/2 C. fresh parsley, chopped
1/4 C. water
2 green onions, chopped
1 tbsp red pepper, diced
1 tbsp dried oregano

1 tbsp paprika
1 tsp bay leaf, very small flakes
1 tsp ground black pepper
1/4 C. red wine vinegar
1/4 C. olive oil

Directions

1. With the mortar and pestle, mash the garlic and salt into a paste.
2. In a bowl, add the onion, parsley, red pepper, garlic paste, oregano, bay leaf, paprika, pepper and water and mix until well combined.
3. Keep aside for about 30 minutes.
4. In the bowl, stir in the vinegar and keep aside for about 30 minutes more.
5. Stir in the oil and refrigerate, covered overnight.

CHIMICHURRI
Linda

Prep Time: 1 hr
Total Time: 1 hr 15 mins

Servings per Recipe: 6
Calories   315.8
Fat   24.3g
Cholesterol   51.4mg
Sodium   45.8mg
Carbohydrates   6.8g
Protein   16.4g

Ingredients
1/2 C. apple cider vinegar
2 tbsp sugar
kosher salt
1 red onion, thinly sliced
1 bunch cilantro, roughly chopped
1 lb. flank steak, trimmed
1 garlic clove

2 tbsp red wine vinegar
1/2 lemon, juice
1/2 tsp red pepper flakes
1/2 C. extra-virgin olive oil
ground black pepper

Directions
1. For the pickled red onion: in a bowl, add the cider vinegar, sugar and 1 tsp of the salt and beat until sugar dissolves.
2. Add the red onion and 2 tbsp of the cilantro and stir to combine well.
3. Keep aside, covered at room temperature for about 1 hour.
4. Meanwhile, in a large bowl of the warm water, soak 20 wooden skewers for at least 20 minutes.
5. Cut the flank steak into 20 (1/8-inch thick) strips against the grain.
6. Thread the steak strips onto skewers in accordion-style.
7. In a blender, add the garlic, remaining cilantro, lemon juice, oil, vinegar, red pepper flakes and 1/2 tsp of the salt and pulse until smooth.
8. Transfer the sauce into a bowl.
9. Season the steak with the salt and black pepper evenly.
10. Grease a grill pan with olive oil and heat over medium-high heat.
11. Arrange the skewers onto the grill pan and cook for about 1 minute per side.
12. Serve the beef skewers alongside the pickled onion and chimichurri sauce.

Hot
Chimichurri Chicken

Prep Time: 15 mins
Total Time: 15 mins

Servings per Recipe: 4
Calories	180.6
Fat	4.0g
Cholesterol	65.8mg
Sodium	376.4mg
Carbohydrates	8.0g
Protein	27.8g

Ingredients

1 C. parsley leaves
1/2 C. cilantro leaves
1 large garlic clove, smashed with the side of a knife and peeled
1/4 C. water
1 tbsp red wine vinegar
2 tsp olive oil
1 tsp lemon juice

1/2 tsp table salt
1/4 tsp black pepper, ground
cooking spray
1 lb. boneless skinless chicken breast
1 medium sweet red pepper, strips
1 medium orange bell pepper, strips
1 medium yellow pepper, strips

Directions

1. In a blender, add the garlic, parsley, cilantro, oil, water, lemon juice, vinegar, salt and pepper and pulse on high speed until a smooth.
2. Grease a grill pan with cooking spray and heat over medium-high heat.
3. Place the chicken and cook for about 3-4 minutes per side.
4. Transfer the chicken onto a platter and cover with a piece of foil to keep warm.
5. Again, grease the grill pan with the cooking spray and heat it.
6. Place the peppers and cook for about 3 minutes per side.
7. Serve the chicken and peppers with a toping of the chimichurri sauce.

ROASTED
2-Vinegar Chimichurri Sauce

Prep Time: 10 mins
Total Time: 2 hr 10 mins

Servings per Recipe: 20
Calories	51.4
Fat	5.4g
Cholesterol	0.0mg
Sodium	572.3mg
Carbohydrates	0.6g
Protein	0.1g

Ingredients
1 1/2 tbsp kosher salt
1/2 C. warm water
1 bunch flat-leaf Italian parsley
3 garlic cloves
1/2 C. extra virgin olive oil
1/2 C. roasted red pepper, coarsely chopped
1 tbsp sweet paprika

1 tbsp oregano, chopped
1 1/2 tsp crushed red pepper flakes
1/2 tsp ground black pepper
1/4 tsp ground cumin
1/4 C. distilled white vinegar
1 tbsp red wine vinegar

Directions
1. In a bowl, dissolve the kosher salt in warm water.
2. Keep aside to cool to room temperature.
3. In a food processor, add the garlic, parsley and olive oil and pulse until chopped.
4. Add the both vinegars, roasted red peppers, oregano, cumin, red pepper, paprika, black pepper and white vinegar and pulse the food processor until a chunky mixture is formed.
5. Place the sauce into a large bowl.
6. Slowly, add the cooled salt water, stirring continuously until well combined.
7. Refrigerate, covered for about 2 hours before serving.

Mediterranean
Latin Lamb

Prep Time: 30 mins
Total Time: 45 mins

Servings per Recipe: 4
Calories	1029.4
Fat	89.5g
Cholesterol	210.9mg
Sodium	457.9mg
Carbohydrates	6.4g
Protein	47.0g

Ingredients

Sauce:
1 C. cilantro leaf, packed
1/2 C. parsley, fresh flat-leaf
2 tbsp mint leaves
1 -2 Serrano chili, halved
3 tbsp rice vinegar
1 tbsp lime juice
1 tbsp honey

1/2 tsp salt
2 tbsp olive oil
Meat:
12 lamb loin chops, trimmed of excess fat
salt & ground black pepper
2 tbsp olive oil
3 tbsp rosemary, chopped
3 garlic cloves, peeled and coarsely chopped

Directions

1. For the chimichurri: in a food processor, add all the ingredients except the oil and pulse until a paste is formed.
2. While the motor is running, slowly add the oil and pulse until smooth.
3. Transfer the chimichurri into a bowl and with a plastic wrap, cover the bowl.
4. Set the broiler of your oven and arrange oven rack at the highest position.
5. Sprinkle the lamb with the salt and pepper evenly.
6. In a large oven-safe skillet, heat the olive oil over high heat and cook the lamb chops for about 10 minutes.
7. Add the garlic and rosemary and cook for about 1-2 minutes.
8. Transfer the skillet into the oven and cook under the broiler for about 5 minutes.
9. Serve the chops with a topping of the chimichurri sauce.

BREAD
in Buenos Aires

Prep Time: 5 mins
Total Time: 30 mins

Servings per Recipe: 1
Calories	1876.8
Fat	45.4g
Cholesterol	0.0mg
Sodium	3525.8mg
Carbohydrates	321.7g
Protein	45.6g

Ingredients

1 3/4 tsp dry yeast
3 C. bread flour
3 tbsp wheat bran
1 tbsp sugar
1 1/2 tsp salt
2 tbsp dried parsley
2 tbsp dried onion

3 garlic cloves
1/4 tsp dried oregano
1/8 tsp cayenne
1/4 tsp rosemary
3 tbsp olive oil
1 1/2 tbsp white wine vinegar
1 C. water

Directions

1. In the bread machine pan, place all the ingredients in the order recommended by the manufacturer.
2. Select the Bread Cycle and press the On Button.
3. Transfer the dough into a well-greased loaf pan.
4. Cover the loaf pan and keep aside for about 30-45 minutes.
5. Set your oven to 400 degrees F.
6. Cook in the oven for about 20-25 minutes.
7. Remove from the oven and coat the top with the butter evenly.

Spicy
Parsley Chimichurri

Prep Time: 5 mins
Total Time: 5 mins

Servings per Recipe: 6
Calories	348.8
Fat	36.5g
Cholesterol	0.0mg
Sodium	337.4mg
Carbohydrates	5.3g
Protein	2.2g

Ingredients

1 3/4 C. flat-leaf Italian parsley, chopped
1 C. olive oil
1/4 C. red wine vinegar
2 tbsp dried oregano
1 tsp ground cumin
1 tsp kosher salt

1 tbsp garlic, minced
1/2 tsp hot sauce
1/4 tsp red pepper flakes
1 tbsp lemon juice

Directions

1. In a food processor, add all the ingredients and pulse until a smooth paste is formed.

SOUTH AMERICAN
Corn with Argentinian Flavored Butter Glaze

Prep Time: 10 mins
Total Time: 1 hr 10 mins

Servings per Recipe: 6
Calories	405.0
Fat	32.3g
Cholesterol	81.3mg
Sodium	28.6mg
Carbohydrates	30.9g
Protein	4.5g

Ingredients
2 tbsp sherry wine vinegar
1 tbsp lemon juice
3/4 C. chopped flat leaf parsley
3 tbsp chopped oregano leaves
2 garlic cloves, roughly chopped
1 pinch red pepper flakes
1 C. unsalted butter, at room temperature

salt
6 ears corn, husked
grated Cotija cheese
lime wedge

Directions
1. For the chimichurri: in a food processor, add the lemon juice, vinegar, garlic, oregano, parsley and red pepper flakes and pulse until garlic and herbs are chopped finely.
2. Place the mixture in the center of a cheesecloth piece and squeeze out the excess liquid.
3. Now, transfer the mixture into a small bowl.
4. Add the butter and stir until well combined.
5. Place the chimichurri butter onto a sheet of a plastic wrap.
6. Carefully, roll the plastic sheet around the butter to form a sausage shape log and then twist the ends to seal.
7. Refrigerate until butter log is set.
8. Meanwhile, in a large pan of the salted boiling water, boil the corn for about 5- minutes.
9. Drain the corn well and arrange onto a serving platter.
10. Remove the butter log from the refrigerator and cut into desired slices.
11. Place 1 slice of chimichurri butter on each ear of corn and serve with a sprinkling of the Cotija cheese alongside the lime wedge.

Top
Sirloin Chimichurri

Prep Time: 10 mins
Total Time: 26 mins

Servings per Recipe: 4
Calories	134.5
Fat	13.6g
Cholesterol	0.0mg
Sodium	301.2mg
Carbohydrates	2.7g
Protein	0.7g

Ingredients
1 C. parsley leaves
1 shallot, coarsely chopped
3 garlic cloves, chopped
3 tbsp red wine vinegar
1/4 C. olive oil

1/2 tsp salt
1/2 tsp black pepper
1 lb. boneless top sirloin steak

Directions
1. Set your gas grill to medium-high heat and lightly, grease the grill grate.
2. In a food processor, add the shallot, garlic, parsley, olive oil, vinegar, 1/4 tsp of the salt and 1/4 tsp of the pepper and pulse until well combined.
3. Season the steak with the remaining salt and pepper evenly.
4. Cook the steak onto the grill for about 8 minutes per side.
5. Transfer the steak in a glass baking dish and top with the sauce evenly.
6. With a piece of foil, cover the baking dish and keep aside for about 5 minutes.
7. Transfer the steak onto a cutting board and with a sharp knife, cut into desired sized slices.
8. Serve the steak slices alongside the remaining sauce.

GLAZED SWEET
Potatoes with Balsamic Dijon Chicken

🥣 Prep Time: 30 mins
🕐 Total Time: 50 mins

Servings per Recipe: 4
Calories	577.8
Fat	28.9g
Cholesterol	114.2mg
Sodium	743.9mg
Carbohydrates	38.2g
Protein	41.5g

Ingredients

Dijon Glazed Chicken:
5 tbsp dark brown sugar
3 tbsp Dijon mustard
2 tbsp hoisin sauce
2 tsp balsamic vinegar
1/2 C. lime juice
1 1/2 lb. boneless skinless chicken breasts
Sauce:
1 C. fresh cilantro
6 tbsp olive oil
3 large garlic cloves
1/4 tsp salt

1/8 tsp pepper
Glazed Sweet Potato:
2 large sweet potatoes
2 tbsp butter
1 1/2 tsp lime juice
1 tsp chipotle chile in adobo
1 tsp adobo sauce
3/4 tsp ground cumin
1/2 tsp ground lemon zest
1/4 tsp salt
1/8 tsp pepper

Directions

1. For the marinade: in a bowl, add the mustard, sugar, lime juice, hoisin sauce and vinegar and mix until well combined.
2. In a small bowl, reserve 6 tbsp of the marinade.
3. In a Zip lock bag, add the remaining marinade and chicken cubes.
4. Shake the bag o coat well.
5. Refrigerate for about 20-30 minutes.
6. Meanwhile, for sweet potatoes: in a medium pan, add the sweet potato chunks and enough water to cover and bring to a boil.
7. Reduce the heat and cook, covered for about 15 minutes.
8. Drain the sweet potato chunks, reserving 1/4 C. of the cooking liquid.
9. In the same pan, add the sweet potato chunks and enough reserved cooking liquid and mash slightly.
10. Add the remaining ingredients and mash until desired consistency is archived.
11. Remove the chicken from the bag and discard the marinade.

12. Thread the chicken onto the skewers.
13. Set your grill and grease the grill grate.
14. Cook the skewers onto the grill until desired doneness, coating with the reserved marinade in the last few minutes of cooking.
15. Meanwhile, for the chimichurri sauce: in a food processor, add the garlic and cilantro and pulse until chopped.
16. While the motor is running, slowly, add the oil and pulse until well combined.
17. Add the salt and pepper and pulse until well combined.
18. Carefully, remove the chicken from the skewers and transfer onto a serving platter alongside smoky sweet potato mash.
19. Top with the chimichurri sauce and serve.

RAFAEL'S
Rib Eye on a Watercress Bed

🥣 Prep Time: 10 mins
🕐 Total Time: 30 mins

Servings per Recipe: 1
Calories	1690.7
Fat	163.7g
Cholesterol	136.0mg
Sodium	202.2mg
Carbohydrates	20.6g
Protein	41.7g

Ingredients
Sauce:
1 bunch flat leaf parsley, leaves only
3 garlic cloves, peeled
3 tbsp red wine vinegar
1/2 lime, juice
3 tbsp chopped oregano leaves
1 tsp ground cumin
1 tsp smoked paprika
120 ml extra virgin olive oil
1 red chili pepper, halved and seeded
salt and ground black pepper
Rib Eye:

1 (200 g) rib eye steaks
1 tbsp oil
Bed and Garnishing:
1 bunch watercress
cooked potato, sautéed with
ground cumin

Directions
1. For the steak: coat the steak with the oil evenly and then, sprinkle with the salt and pepper generously.
2. Heat a lightly greased skillet and cook the steak for about 2-3 minutes per side.
3. Meanwhile, for the chimichurri relish: in a food processor, add all the ingredients and pulse until a coarse paste is formed.
4. Transfer the steak onto a platter for about 5 minutes before serving.
5. Top the steak with the chimichurri relish and serve alongside the watercress and sautéed potatoes.

Chimichurri
Steak Picnic

Prep Time: 10 mins
Total Time: 20 mins

Servings per Recipe: 4
Calories   672.1
Fat   49.4g
Cholesterol   154.2mg
Sodium   716.1mg
Carbohydrates   5.8g
Protein   49.2g

Ingredients
1 tbsp vegetable oil
1 large red onion, cut into rounds
salt & pepper
2 - 3 lb. flank steaks
chimichurri sauce
1 C. parsley, packed

5 garlic cloves, peeled
1/2 C. olive oil
1/4 C. red wine vinegar
1/4 tsp red pepper flakes
1 tsp table salt

Directions
1. Set your grill according to manufacturer's directions.
2. Arrange the onion rounds onto a baking sheet.
3. Coat the onion rounds with the oil lightly and then sprinkle with the salt and pepper.
4. Season the steak with the salt and pepper evenly.
5. Arrange the steak and onion rounds onto the grill.
6. Cook the onion onto the grill for about 10-12 minutes, flipping once half way through.
7. Cook the steak onto the grill for about 5-7 minutes.
8. Flip and cook for about 2-5 minutes further.
9. Remove from the grill and transfer the steak onto a cutting board.
10. With a piece of the foil, cover the steak for about 5 minutes.
11. Meanwhile, for he chimichurri sauce: in a food processor, fitted with a steel blade, add the garlic
12. and parsley and pulse until finely chopped.
13. Transfer the mixture into a bowl with the remaining sauce ingredients and beat until well combined.
14. With a sharp knife, cut the steak into slices against the grain and sprinkle with the salt and black pepper.
15. Arrange the onion rounds onto a platter and top with the steak slices.
16. Serve alongside the Chimichurri Sauce.

Mason Jar
Chimichurri

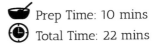 Prep Time: 10 mins

Total Time: 22 mins

Servings per Recipe: 1

Calories	372.9
Fat	36.6g
Cholesterol	0.0mg
Sodium	782.4mg
Carbohydrates	8.6g
Protein	1.3g

Ingredients

1 chopped sweet pepper
1 chopped skinned and seeded tomatoes
1 chopped onion
2 cloves chopped garlic
2 chopped bay leaves
2 tbsp chopped parsley

1/2 C. oil
1 C. vinegar
1 tsp salt
1 tsp cracked black peppercorns
1 tsp oregano

Directions

1. In a bowl, add all the ingredients and mix until well combined.
2. Refrigerate, covered for about 12 hours before serving.

New York
Steakhouse Steaks

Prep Time: 45 mins
Total Time: 1 hr 5 mins

Servings per Recipe: 6
Calories	378.2
Fat	27.7g
Cholesterol	107.1mg
Sodium	384.0mg
Carbohydrates	2.9g
Protein	27.8g

Ingredients
3 tbsp fruity olive oil, divided
2 garlic cloves, thinly sliced
2 garlic cloves, pressed
1/4 tsp dry crushed red pepper
1 bay leaf, broken in half
1/3 C. chopped shallot
1/4 C. chopped Italian parsley
2 tbsp pitted kalamata olives, chopped

2 tbsp red wine vinegar
1 - 2 tbsp water
2 (14 - 16 oz.) New York strip steaks
2 tsp paprika
1 tsp kosher salt
1/4 tsp cayenne pepper

Directions
1. In a heavy medium skillet, heat 2 tbsp of the oil over medium heat and sauté the sliced garlic, bay leaf and red pepper for about 1 minute.
2. Add the shallots and sauté for about 2 minutes.
3. Remove from the heat and stir in the olives, parsley, vinegar, salt, pepper and desired amount of the water.
4. Keep aside at room temperature for about 2 hours.
5. Rub each steak with the pressed garlic and then, coat with 1 tbsp of the oil.
6. Season the both steaks with 1/2 tsp of the paprika, cayenne, 1/4 tsp of the coarse salt and black pepper evenly.
7. Keep aide at room temperature for at least 30 minutes or up to 2 hours.
8. Set your oven to 400 degrees F.
9. Heat a heavy, very large greased oven-proof skillet over high heat and cook the steaks for about 5 minutes.
10. Flip the steaks and transfer skillet into the oven.
11. Cook in the oven for about 10 minutes.
12. Remove from the oven and place the steaks onto a cutting board for about 5 minutes.
13. Cut each steak into thin slice cross-wise.
14. Serve the steak slices with a topping of the chimichurri saucer.

HUBBY'S
Favorite Steak

Prep Time: 10 mins
Total Time: 16 mins

Servings per Recipe: 4
Calories	217.5
Fat	11.8g
Cholesterol	77.1mg
Sodium	444.0mg
Carbohydrates	1.8g
Protein	24.6g

Ingredients
Sauce:
2/3 C. flat leaf parsley
2 tbsp green onions, chopped
2 tbsp water
1 tbsp prepared horseradish
1 tbsp red wine vinegar
1 tsp olive oil
1/8 tsp salt

1 garlic clove, peeled
Meat:
1 lb. flank steak, trimmed
1 tsp cumin, ground
1/2 tsp salt
1/4 tsp black pepper
1 tsp olive oil

Directions
1. For the chimichurri sauce: in a food processor, add all the ingredients and pulse until smooth.
2. Place the sauce into a small bowl and keep aside.
3. For the steak, season the steak with the cumin, 1/2 tsp salt, and black pepper evenly.
4. In a large nonstick skillet, heat 1 tsp of the oil over medium-high heat and cook the steak for about 3 minutes per side.
5. remove from the heat and place the steak onto a cutting board for about 5 minutes.
6. With a sharp knife, cut the steak into thin slices diagonally across the grain.
7. Serve the steak slices alongside the with chimichurri sauce.

South American
Surf n Turf

Prep Time: 15 mins
Total Time: 30 mins

Servings per Recipe: 4
Calories	429.5
Fat	30.5g
Cholesterol	90.5mg
Sodium	403.4mg
Carbohydrates	3.7g
Protein	34.3g

Ingredients
1/2 C. olive oil
1/3 C. fresh lime juice
4 garlic cloves, minced
1/2 small onion, chopped
1/4 C. cilantro, chopped
1/2 tsp dried oregano
1/2 tsp salt
1/4 tsp cayenne pepper
1/4 tsp black pepper
4 strips steaks
1 lb. halibut fillet, with skin, cut into 4 pieces

Directions
1. For the chimichurri sauce: in a bowl, add the onion, garlic, cilantro, lime juice, oil, oregano, cayenne, salt and black pepper and mix until well combined,
2. In a zip lock bag, add the steak and 1/3 C. of the chimichurri sauce.
3. Seal the bag and shake to coat well.
4. Cut halibut fillet into 4 serving pieces.
5. In a zip lock bag, add the halibut pieces and 1/3 C. of the chimichurri sauce.
6. Seal the bag and shake to coat well.
7. Reserve remaining 1/3 C. sauce.
8. Refrigerate the both bags for about 30 minutes.
9. Set your outdoor grill with hot coals for direct grilling.
10. Remove the steak and halibut from the bags and discard the marinade.
11. Cook the steak and halibut onto the grill, covered for about 10 minutes, flipping once half way through.
12. Serve steak and fish alongside the reserved chimichurri sauce.

STEAK
in Argentina

Prep Time: 12 mins
Total Time: 20 mins

Servings per Recipe: 4
Calories	438.8
Fat	27.8g
Cholesterol	115.6mg
Sodium	191.5mg
Carbohydrates	7.7g
Protein	37.1g

Ingredients
1 1/2 lb. flank steaks, cut into strips
1/2 C. red wine vinegar
1/4 C. olive oil
3 tbsp tomato paste
2 tbsp garlic, minced
1 tbsp sugar

1 tsp ground cumin
1 tsp ground black pepper
1 tsp red pepper flakes
salt

Directions
1. Set your grill for medium heat and lightly, grease the grill grate.
2. For the chimichurri: in a large bowl, add all the ingredients except steak pieces and beat until well combined.
3. Add the steak strips and coat with the chimichurri generously.
4. Thread the steak strips onto each of 4 metal skewers evenly.
5. Fold the meat slices in the accordion manner and thread 4 metal skewers each with about 4-5 meat slices spearing through the center.
6. Spread the slices throughout the skewer length.
7. Cook the skewers onto the grill, covered for about 3 minutes.
8. Flip and coat the skewers with the chimichurri sauce evenly.
9. Cook the skewers onto the grill, covered for about 3 minutes further.

Chimichurri
Tenderloin

🍳 Prep Time: 25 mins
🕐 Total Time: 45 mins

Servings per Recipe: 4
Calories   352.3
Fat   28.0g
Cholesterol   80.5mg
Sodium   644.1mg
Carbohydrates   3.3g
Protein   20.9g

Ingredients

Meat:
4 (4 oz.) beef tenderloin steaks, trimmed
1/2 tsp salt
1/4 tsp ground black pepper
Chimichurri:
3/4 C. flat leaf parsley
1/4 C. cilantro leaves
1/4 C. mint leaf
1/4 C. chopped onion

1/4 C. reduced-sodium fat-free chicken broth
3 tbsp sherry wine vinegar
2 tbsp oregano leaves
1 tsp olive oil
1/2 tsp salt
1/2 tsp ground black pepper
1/2 tsp crushed red pepper flakes
3 garlic cloves

Directions

1. Soak a plank in water for about 1 hour.
2. Set your grill, one side to medium and another side to high heat.
3. Season the steak with 1/2 tsp of the salt and 1/4 tsp of the black pepper.
4. Place plank onto grill rack over high heat for about 5 minutes.
5. Carefully flip the plank and place over medium heat.
6. Arrange the steak onto charred side of the plank and cook, covered for about 12 minutes
7. For the sauce: in a food processor, add all the ingredients and pulse until smooth.
8. Serve the steak alongside the sauce.

ARGENTINIAN
Tacos with Adobo Aioli

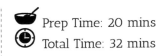

Prep Time: 20 mins
Total Time: 32 mins

Servings per Recipe: 3
Calories	777.0
Fat	52.1g
Cholesterol	119.0mg
Sodium	539.2mg
Carbohydrates	36.2g
Protein	38.4g

Ingredients
Sauce:
1 small bunch cilantro
1/2 medium yellow onion
lime juice
1/2 tsp crushed red pepper flakes
Aioli:
4 oz. sour cream
1 large chipotle chile in adobo
Tacos:
6 small flour tortillas, warmed
1 lb. skirt steak
7 garlic cloves, divided

1 tsp Dijon mustard
1/4 C. olive oil
2 tbsp olive oil
1/3 C. red wine vinegar
2 tbsp red wine vinegar
kosher salt
ground black pepper

Directions
1. In a bag, place the steak, 3 garlic cloves, Dijon mustard, 2 tbsp each oil and vinegar, 1 tsp of the salt and 1/2 tsp of the black pepper and rub the mixture with the steak generously.
2. Refrigerate to marinate for about 2 hours.
3. Remove the meat from the bag and with paper towels, pat dry to remove any excess moisture.
4. Season the steak with the salt and pepper evenly.
5. Set your indoor grill for medium-high heat and lightly, grease the grill grate.
6. Cook the steak onto the grill for about 6 minutes per side.
7. Place the steak onto a cutting board and cover with a piece of foil for about 10 minutes..
8. With a sharp knife, cut into thin slices across the grain.

Villa Maria
Wet Marinade

🍲 Prep Time: 15 mins
🕐 Total Time: 15 mins

Servings per Recipe: 1
Calories   1371.7
Fat   145.3g
Cholesterol   0.0mg
Sodium   99.1mg
Carbohydrates   18.3g
Protein   5.9g

Ingredients

2 C. parsley, firmly packed
1/4 C. oregano leaves
3 -6 garlic cloves
2 tbsp chopped onions

1/2 C. olive oil
2 tbsp red wine vinegar
1 tbsp lime juice
salt and red pepper flakes

Directions

1. In a food processor, add the onion and garlic and pulse until finely chopped.
2. Add the parsley and oregano and pulse until finely chopped.
3. Transfer the mixture into a bowl and stir in the olive oil, vinegar, lime juice, salt and red pepper until well combined.
4. Refrigerate to store before using.

SAN FERNANDO
Spring Rolls

Prep Time: 30 mins
Total Time: 45 mins

Servings per Recipe: 1
Calories	111.4
Fat	9.3g
Cholesterol	0.0mg
Sodium	130.3mg
Carbohydrates	6.9g
Protein	1.3g

Ingredients

1 C. shredded romaine lettuce
3 coarsely shredded carrots
1/2 C. bite-size strips zucchini
1/2 C. bite-size strips peeled jicama
2 green onions, strips
6 sheets rice paper
6 sprigs flat-leaf parsley
Sauce:

1 1/2 C. lightly packed flat-leaf parsley
1/4 C. olive oil
1/4 C. rice vinegar
6 garlic cloves, minced
1/4 tsp salt
1/4 tsp ground black pepper
1/4 tsp crushed red pepper flakes

Directions

1. For the sauce: in a food processor, add all the ingredients and pulse until finely chopped.
2. In a large bowl, add the vegetable and half of the sauce and mix well.
3. Keep aside for about 25-30 minutes, stirring occasionally.
4. Refrigerate, covered the remaining sauce before using.
5. In a pie plate, place the warm water.
6. Carefully, dip 1 rice paper into the water and immediately, transfer onto a clean kitchen towel.
7. Keep aside for a few seconds.
8. Arrange 1 parsley sprig into the middle of the paper and top with 1/3 C. of the vegetable mixture just below the center.
9. Roll up the rice paper from bottom tightly, tucking in one side as while rolling.
10. Repeat with the remaining spring rolls.
11. Serve alongside the remaining sauce.

Argentinian Tofu

Prep Time: 10 mins
Total Time: 20 mins

Servings per Recipe: 4
Calories   148.3
Fat   11.6g
Cholesterol   0.0mg
Sodium   22.5mg
Carbohydrates   3.7g
Protein   9.8g

Ingredients

16 oz. extra firm tofu, drained and chopped
2 tbsp oregano
1 C. parsley
2 cloves garlic, peeled

1/4 tsp hot red pepper flakes
3 tbsp white wine vinegar
2 tbsp extra virgin olive oil
salt

Directions

1. In a food processor, add the garlic, parsley, oregano, salt and pepper flakes and pulse until finely minced.
2. Add the 1 tbsp of the oil and vinegar and pulse until a rough sauce is formed.
3. Transfer the sauce into a bowl.
4. Set your grill for medium heat and lightly, grease the grill grate.
5. Coat the tofu slices with remaining olive oil.
6. Cook the tofu onto the grill for about 5 minutes per side.
7. Serve the tofu slices with a topping of the sauce.

CHIMICHURRI
Matchstick Skillet

Prep Time: 4 hr 15 mins
Total Time: 4 hr 30 mins

Servings per Recipe: 2
Calories	735.4
Fat	45.1g
Cholesterol	217.9mg
Sodium	997.4mg
Carbohydrates	5.1g
Protein	73.6g

Ingredients
1 1/2 lb. boneless skinless chicken breasts,
cut in strips
1 C. minced parsley
3 cloves garlic, minced
1/3 C. olive oil
1/4 C. red wine vinegar
2 tbsp lemon juice

1/2 tsp salt
1/2 tsp coarse grind black pepper
1/2 tsp dried oregano
1/4 tsp cayenne pepper

Directions
1. In a plastic zip lock bag, add all the ingredients.
2. Seal the bag and shake to coat well.
3. Refrigerate to marinate for at least 4 hours.
4. Remove the chicken from the bag discard the remaining marinade.
5. Heat a greased pan and cook the chicken strips for about 5 minutes per side.

Scallops
in Argentina

Prep Time: 10 mins

Total Time: 15 mins

Servings per Recipe: 4
Calories   232.6
Fat   5.0g
Cholesterol   56.2mg
Sodium   574.0mg
Carbohydrates   16.4g
Protein   29.9g

Ingredients

1 1/2 C. loosely packed mint leaves
3/4 C. sliced green onion
2 tbsp water
1 1/2 tbsp lime juice
1 tbsp honey
1 tsp minced seeded serrano chili
1/2 tsp salt
1/2 tsp ground black pepper
1 garlic clove

3 tbsp yellow cornmeal
1 1/2 lb. sea scallops
1 tbsp olive oil
green onion, strips

Directions

1. In a food processor, add the green onion, garlic, mint, Serrano chili, water, lime juice, honey, salt
2. and black pepper and pulse until finely chopped.
3. In a shallow dish, place the cornmeal.
4. Coat the scallops with the cornmeal.
5. In a large nonstick skillet, heat the oil over medium-high heat and cook the scallops for about 3 minutes per side.
6. Serve the scallops with a garnishing of the onion strips alongside the chimichurri.

CHIMICHURRI
Beef Cakes

Prep Time: 15 mins
Total Time: 30 mins

Servings per Recipe: 4
Calories   350.8
Fat   22.6g
Cholesterol   126.9mg
Sodium   441.6mg
Carbohydrates   9.7g
Protein   26.2g

Ingredients

Beef Cakes:
1 egg, beaten
2/3 C. corn flakes, crushed
1/3 C. Spanish onion, minced
1/3 C. light sour cream
3 cloves garlic, smashed
1 tbsp parsley, chopped
1/4 tsp salt
1/4 tsp pepper
1 lb. lean ground beef
1 tsp vegetable oil
Sauce:

1 C. parsley, packed
2 tbsp oregano, packed
2 tbsp extra virgin olive oil
1 tbsp red wine vinegar
1 jalapeño pepper, seeded
2 cloves garlic, chopped
1/4 tsp salt
1/4 tsp pepper

Directions

1. For the patties: in a bowl, add all the ingredients and mix until well combined.
2. Make 4 (1/2-inch thick) patties from the mixture.
3. In nonstick frying pan, heat the oil over medium-high heat and cook the patties for about 5 minutes per side.
4. Meanwhile, for the chimichurri sauce: in a food processor, add all the ingredients and pulse until processor finely chopped.
5. Serve the patties with a topping of the sauce.

Red
Chimichurri
Marinade

Prep Time: 5 mins
Total Time: 6 mins

Servings per Recipe: 1

Calories	571.5
Fat	57.7g
Cholesterol	0.0mg
Sodium	1179.9mg
Carbohydrates	17.9g
Protein	4.1g

Ingredients

4 tbsp virgin olive oil
1 1/2 tbsp hot paprika
2 tbsp cayenne
4 garlic cloves, minced
1 tsp ground black pepper

1 tsp cumin, toasted and ground
1 bay leaf, broken in half
1/2 tsp kosher salt

Directions

1. In a bowl, add all the ingredients and mix until well combined.
2. Place in a jar to preserve.

CHIMICHURRI
Pesto

Prep Time: 10 mins
Total Time: 10 mins

Servings per Recipe: 4
Calories	253.1
Fat	27.1g
Cholesterol	0.0mg
Sodium	150.5mg
Carbohydrates	3.0g
Protein	0.7g

Ingredients
1/4 C. basil leaves, chopped
1/4 C. flat leaf parsley, chopped
1 tsp oregano, chopped
1/2 C. extra virgin olive oil
1/4 C. red wine vinegar
2 garlic cloves, minced

2 dried red chilies
1/4 tsp coarse salt
1/8 tsp ground pepper

Directions
1. In a bowl, add all the ingredients and mix until well combined.
2. Transfer into an airtight container and store in refrigerator up to 3 days.

Burgers
with Chimichurri Seasoning

Prep Time: 30 mins
Total Time: 48 mins

Servings per Recipe: 6
Calories	474.9
Fat	26.4g
Cholesterol	98.2mg
Sodium	605.0mg
Carbohydrates	22.5g
Protein	34.8g

Ingredients
1 tbsp ground cumin
1 C. cilantro leaves, lightly packed
1 C. Italian parsley, lightly packed
2 tbsp white wine vinegar
1 tsp crushed red pepper flakes
1/2 tsp sea salt
1/4 C. canola oil
2 lb. lean ground beef
1/4 tsp salt

1/4 tsp ground red pepper
6 hamburger buns, split and toasted
sliced tomatoes
sliced onion

Directions
1. Set your grill for medium heat and lightly, grease the grill grate.
2. Heat a small skillet over low heat and toast the cumin for about 2 minutes, stirring continuously.
3. Immediately, remove from the heat.
4. For the chimichurri, in a blender, add the parsley, cilantro, vinegar, red pepper and salt and pulse on lowest speed until just combined.
5. While the motor is running, slowly add the oil until well combined.
6. In a large bowl, add the ground beef, the 1/4 tsp salt and ground red pepper and mix well.
7. Make 12 (3 1/2-inch) patties from the mixture.
8. Place about 1 tbsp of the chimichurri mixture in the middle of each of 6 of patties.
9. Top each with the remaining patties and press the edges to seal.
10. Arrange the patties onto the grill over direct heat and cook for about 18-22 minutes, flip once halfway through.
11. Coat each roll with some of the chimichurri sauce and top each with burgers, followed by the remaining sauce, tomatoes and onions.

PEÑO
Chimichurri

Prep Time: 10 mins
Total Time: 10 mins

Servings per Recipe: 16
Calories   98.1
Fat   10.2g
Cholesterol   0.0mg
Sodium   224.1mg
Carbohydrates   1.8g
Protein   0.4g

Ingredients
1 bunch cilantro
1 bunch flat leaf parsley
1 shallot
1 jalapeño
6 garlic cloves
6 tbsp lime juice
3 tbsp red wine vinegar
2 tsp dried oregano

1/2 tsp cumin
1 1/2 tsp sea salt
1/2 tsp ground pepper
3/4 C. extra virgin olive oil

Directions
1. In a food processor, add all the ingredients except the oil and pulse until well combined.
2. While the motor is running, slowly add the oil until a slightly chunky mixture is formed.

Chimichurri Steak 101

🥄 Prep Time: 10 mins
🕐 Total Time: 28 mins

Servings per Recipe: 4	
Calories	668.1
Fat	47.1g
Cholesterol	117.0mg
Sodium	1253.8mg
Carbohydrates	5.0g
Protein	54.2g

Ingredients

1/2 C. extra virgin olive oil
2/3 C. vinegar
2 tbsp lemon juice
1 C. chopped flat leaf parsley
4 tbsp chopped basil leaves
1 tbsp chopped oregano leaves

3 tbsp minced garlic
2 tbsp minced shallots
3/4 tsp cracked black pepper
2 1/2 tsp kosher salt
1/4 tsp crushed red pepper flakes
1 (1 3/4-2 lb.) skirt steaks

Directions

1. In a food processor, add the shallots, garlic, oregano, parsley, lemon juice, vinegar, olive oil, 1/2 tsp of the salt, 1/4 tsp of the black pepper and red pepper flakes and pulse until well combined.
2. In a non-reactive bowl, reserve 1 C. of the chimichurri sauce and keep aside, covered for up to 6 hours.
3. Season the steak with 1 tsp of the salt and 1/4 tsp of the black pepper evenly.
4. In a large re-sealable plastic bag, add the steak and remaining chimichurri sauce.
5. Seal the bag and shake to coat well.
6. Refrigerate for at least 2-4 hours.
7. Set your grill for medium heat and lightly, grease the grill grate.
8. Remove the steak from the refrigerator and keep aside to in room temperature for about 30 minutes before cooking.
9. Remove the steak from the bag, keeping the excess sauce aside.
10. Coat the steak with the excess chimichurri sauce evenly and cook onto the grill for about 6 minutes.
11. Rotate the steak to 45 degrees and cook for about 6 minutes.
12. Flip the steak and cook for about 6-8 minutes.
13. Place the steak onto a cutting board for about 5-7 minutes before slicing..
14. Cut the steak into 2-inch wide strips across the grain.
15. Serve the steak slice alongside the reserved chimichurri sauce.

BURGERS
Santa Domingo

Prep Time: 30 mins
Total Time: 45 mins

Servings per Recipe: 4
Calories	621.4
Fat	45.6g
Cholesterol	161.1mg
Sodium	163.4mg
Carbohydrates	10.2g
Protein	40.7g

Ingredients
2 lb. lean ground beef
2 C. chopped cabbage
1 large red onion
mustard
mayonnaise
ketchup, sliced
1 tomatoes, sliced
1 avocado, peeled, pitted and sliced

4 -6 Portuguese rolls
1 large green pepper
6 garlic cloves
1 tbsp oregano
olive oil
2 (1 oz.) packages Goya sazon

Directions
1. In a food processor, add the green pepper, garlic, oregano and a tbsp of the olive oil and pulse until smooth.
2. In a large bowl, add he ground beef, seasoning packages, 2 tbsp of the pureed mixture, salt and black pepper and mix until well combined.
3. Make oval shaped and equal sized patties from the beef mixture.
4. Heat a 12-inch cast iron frying pan and cook the patties until cooked through.
5. Spread the mayonnaise on the rolls and top with patties, followed by the tomatoes, onions and avocado.
6. Serve with a drizzling of the ketchup and mustard.

Rosa's
Shrimp Rice

Prep Time: 25 mins
Total Time: 30 mins

Servings per Recipe: 4
Calories	420.7
Fat	21.7g
Cholesterol	143.2mg
Sodium	1084.0mg
Carbohydrates	35.6g
Protein	18.9g

Ingredients

1 C. lightly packed cilantro leaf
2 red jalapeño chiles, seeded
2 garlic cloves, peeled
2 - 3 tbsp red wine vinegar
6 tbsp olive oil, divided

3/4 tsp salt
1/4 tsp pepper
1 lb. medium shrimp, peeled and deveined
3 C. hot cooked long-grain rice

Directions

1. Set the broiler of your oven and arrange oven rack about 4-inch from the heating element.
2. In a food processor, add the garlic, cilantro, jalapeños, 1/4 C. of the oil, vinegar, salt and pepper and pulse until smooth.
3. Transfer the sauce into a bowl and keep aside.
4. In a bowl, add the shrimp and remaining 2 tbsp of the oil and toss to coat well.
5. Arrange the shrimp onto a broiler pan and cook under the broiler for about 2 minutes per side.
6. In a bowl, add the hot rice and half of the sauce and mix well.
7. arrange the rice and shrimp onto a platter and serve with a topping of the remaining sauce.

5-INGREDIENT
Mushroom and Steak Kebabs

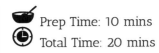 Prep Time: 10 mins

Total Time: 20 mins

Servings per Recipe: 6
Calories	168.0
Fat	4.4g
Cholesterol	56.7mg
Sodium	68.7mg
Carbohydrates	8.2g
Protein	24.6g

Ingredients
1 (20 oz.) packages Simply Potatoes Red
Potato Wedges
3/4 C. prepared chimichurri sauce
1 1/4 lb. boneless beef top sirloin steaks, cut
into cubes
1 medium red onion, cut into wedges
12 baby portabella mushrooms

Directions
1. In a 2-quart microwave-safe bowl, add the potato wedges and water and microwave covered on High for about 4 minutes
2. Drain the potatoes well and keep aside to cool slightly.
3. In a 1 gallon plastic re-sealable bag, add the beef, cooled potatoes, mushrooms, onion and chimichurri sauce.
4. Seal the bag and gently, shake to coat.
5. Refrigerate for about 30 minutes.
6. Set your gas grill to medium heat.
7. Thread the beef, potatoes, mushrooms and onion onto 6 pre-soaked wooden skewers.
8. Cook the skewers onto the grill for about 10 minutes, flipping once half way through.
9. Serve with a drizzling of the additional chimichurri sauce.

Peruvian
Paprika Chimichurri Marinade

Prep Time: 5 mins
Total Time: 5 mins

Servings per Recipe: 1
Calories	992.5
Fat	108.1g
Cholesterol	0.0mg
Sodium	1563.3mg
Carbohydrates	6.1g
Protein	1.2g

Ingredients

1 bunch parsley, roughly chopped
8 garlic cloves, crushed
1 tsp oregano
2 tbsp paprika
1/4-1/2 tsp cayenne pepper

1 - 2 tsp salt
1/3 C. red wine vinegar
3/4 C. olive oil

Directions

1. In a blender, add the vinegar, garlic, parsley, oregano, paprika, cayenne and salt and pulse until a chunky mixture is formed.
2. Transfer the mixture into a bowl.
3. Add the oil and stir to combine well.
4. Keep aside for least 30 minutes.

CHIMICHURRI
Rub

Prep Time: 5 mins
Total Time: 5 mins

Servings per Recipe: 1
Calories   101.5
Fat   1.7g
Cholesterol   0.0mg
Sodium   4764.5mg
Carbohydrates   21.6g
Protein   4.6g

Ingredients

1 tbsp dried parsley
1 tbsp dried onion flakes
1 tsp dried oregano
1 tsp dry garlic granules
1 tsp red chili pepper flakes
1 tsp dry basil

1 tsp paprika
1/2 tsp bay laurel powder
1 tsp salt

Directions

1. In a spice grinder, add all the ingredients and grind until powdered finely.

Latin
Bruschetta

Prep Time: 10 mins
Total Time: 10 mins

Servings per Recipe: 6
Calories   258.7
Fat   19.7g
Cholesterol   0.0mg
Sodium   467.9mg
Carbohydrates   19.6g
Protein   3.4g

Ingredients

2 tbsp lemon juice
2 tbsp red wine vinegar
3 garlic cloves, minced
3/4 tsp salt
1/2 tsp red pepper flakes
1/2 tsp dried oregano
1/4 tsp ground black pepper
1/4 C. olive oil
1/4 C. chopped cilantro

1/4 C. chopped parsley
2 avocados, peeled, pitted and cubed
6 slices bread

Directions

1. In a bowl, add the garlic, vinegar, lemon juice, oregano salt, red pepper flakes and black pepper and mix until well combined.
2. Add the oil and beat until well combined.
3. Add the parsley and cilantro and stir to combine.
4. Gently, fold in the avocado cubes.
5. To the toast slices with the avocado mixture and serve.

CITRUS
Chimichurri

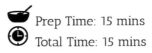 Prep Time: 15 mins

Total Time: 15 mins

Servings per Recipe: 12
Calories	47.8
Fat	4.5g
Cholesterol	0.0mg
Sodium	5.8mg
Carbohydrates	1.7g
Protein	0.4g

Ingredients
1 1/2 C. cilantro, trimmed stems
1 1/2 C. flat leaf parsley, trimmed stems
4 garlic cloves, chopped roughly
2 small limes, juice
1 small shallot, chopped roughly
1/4 C. extra virgin olive oil

1 1/2 tbsp red wine vinegar
1 1/2 tbsp white wine vinegar
1 jalapeño
sea salt
ground pepper

Directions
1. In a blender, add all the ingredients and pulse until smooth.

Chimichurri
Marinade Sirloin

🥘 Prep Time: 40 mins
🕐 Total Time: 1 hr

Servings per Recipe: 6
Calories	551.5
Fat	46.9g
Cholesterol	101.3mg
Sodium	441.6mg
Carbohydrates	2.6g
Protein	29.3g

Ingredients

2 lb. boneless beef sirloin
Sauce:
2/3 C. olive oil
1/3 C. parsley, minced
1/3 C. cayenne pepper sauce

3 tbsp lemon juice
1 tbsp Worcestershire sauce
2 tsp dried oregano leaves
4 garlic cloves, peeled & crushed

Directions

1. For the marinade: in a food processor, add all the ingredients and pulse until well combined.
2. In a bowl, reserve about 2/3 C. of the marinade mixture.
3. With a sharp knife, make 1/8-1/4-inch deep cut on both sides of the steak.
4. In large re-sealable plastic bag, add the steak and remaining marinade mixture.
5. Seal bag and shake to cover well.
6. Refrigerate to marinate for at least 30 minutes.
7. Remove the steak from the bag and discard the marinade.
8. Cook the steak onto the grill over hot coals for about 10 minutes per side.
9. Remove from the grill and lace the steak onto the cutting board for about 5 minutes.
10. Cut the steak into slices diagonally.
11. Serve the steak slices alongside the reserved sauce.

GLAZED
Chicken & Green Beans

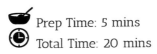 Prep Time: 5 mins
Total Time: 20 mins

Servings per Recipe: 4
Calories	258.9
Fat	11.9g
Cholesterol	68.4mg
Sodium	89.4mg
Carbohydrates	10.2g
Protein	29.5g

Ingredients
4 boneless skinless chicken breast halves
3 tbsp cooking oil
12 oz. young green beans
3/4 C. packed Italian parsley
1 tbsp cider vinegar

2 garlic cloves, halved
1/4 tsp crushed red pepper flakes
1 lemon

Directions
1. Brush chicken with 1 tbsp of the oil; sprinkle 1/4 tsp each salt and black pepper.
2. Grill chicken on rack directly over medium heat for 12 to 15 minutes or until no longer pink, turning once halfway through grilling time.
3. In a 1-1/2-quart microwave-safe dish, place the beans and 1 tbsp of the water.
4. With a vented plastic wrap, cover the dish and microwave on High for about 3 minutes.
5. Drain the beans well.
6. For the chimichurri sauce: in a small food processor, add the garlic, parsley, vinegar, remaining oil, 1/4 tsp of the salt and red pepper and
7. pulse until almost smooth.
8. Divide the chicken and beans onto the serving plates and top with the chimichurri sauce and lemon peel.
9. Serve with a drizzling of the lemon juice.

5-Ingredient
Chimichurri

🥄 Prep Time: 15 mins
🕐 Total Time: 15 mins

Servings per Recipe: 1
Calories	1018.0
Fat	108.7g
Cholesterol	0.0mg
Sodium	55.0mg
Carbohydrates	10.4g
Protein	3.3g

Ingredients

3 bunches curly-leaf parsley, finely chopped
6 tbsp garlic, minced
2 C. extra virgin olive oil

1 C. white vinegar
salt & ground black pepper

Directions

1. In a medium bowl, add all the ingredients and beat until well combined
2. Keep aside for about 2 hours before serving.

DINNER
in Argentina
(Chimichurri Chicken &
Long Grain)

Prep Time: 30 mins
Total Time: 1 hr 10 mins

Servings per Recipe: 6
Calories   719.7
Fat   49.0g
Cholesterol   92.8mg
Sodium   400.6mg
Carbohydrates   33.5g
Protein   35.4g

Ingredients

Sauce:
10 garlic cloves, peeled
1 bunch flat leaf parsley, stemmed
3/4 C. olive oil
1/4 C. white balsamic vinegar
1/4 C. chicken broth
3/4 tsp dried oregano
3/4 tsp dried basil
1/2 small red chili pepper, seeded and diced
salt & ground black pepper
Meat:

3 whole chicken breasts, halved, boned and flattened
2 tbsp olive oil
Long Grain:
3 tbsp shredded coconut
3 tbsp dried currants
1 tbsp olive oil
1 C. long grained white rice
2 C. chicken broth
salt & ground black pepper
2 slices limes

Directions

1. For the sauce; in a food processor, add the garlic and pulse until pureed.
2. Add the chili pepper and parsley and pulse until finely chopped.
3. Add the broth, vinegar, oil and seasonings and pulse until well combined.
4. In a zip lock bag, mix together 3 tbsp of the chimichurri sauce and the 2 tbsp of the oil.
5. Add the chicken breasts and coat with the mixture generously.
6. Seal the bag and refrigerate for at least 30 minutes or up to 4 hours.
7. Set your grill for medium heat and lightly, grease the grill grate.
8. Remove the chicken from the bag.
9. Cook the chicken onto the grill for bout 7-10 minutes per side.
10. Remove from the grill and place onto a platter.
11. With a piece of the foil, cover the chicken to keep warm.
12. Meanwhile, for the rice: heat a medium non-stick pan over medium heat and toast the coconut for about 2-3 minutes, stirring continuously.
13. Place the coconut into a bowl and keep aside.
14. In the same pan, heat the oil over medium-high heat and sauté the rice for about 3 minutes.
15. Stir in the broth and bring to a boil.
16. Add the lime slices, salt and pepper and with a fork, stir well.
17. Reduce the heat to low and simmer, covered for about 15-20 minutes.
18. Add the currants and toasted coconut and with a fork, stir well.
19. Divide the rice onto 6 hot serving plates, followed by a chicken breast.
20. Serve with a topping of the remaining chimichurri sauce.

Black Bean
Pizzas with Chimichurri

🥣 Prep Time: 25 mins
🕐 Total Time: 1 hr 48 mins

Servings per Recipe: 1
Calories   126.7
Fat   2.9g
Cholesterol   2.7mg
Sodium   298.4mg
Carbohydrates   20.8g
Protein   4.3g

Ingredients

1 red bell pepper, halved and seeded
1 tbsp cornmeal
1 tbsp dry yeast
1/8 tsp sugar
1 C. warm water, divided
3 C. flour
1 tsp salt
1/2 C. finely grated Parmesan cheese
Beans:
1/2 C. coarsely chopped onion

1 (15 oz.) cans sodium black beans, rinsed and drained
1 (14 1/2 oz.) cans organic fire-roasted diced tomatoes and green chilies
Sauce:
1/4 C. chopped fresh parsley
1/4 C. chopped fresh cilantro
2 tbsp olive oil
1 tbsp fresh lemon juice
2 tsp minced garlic

Directions

1. Set the broiler of your oven and line a baking sheet with a piece of the foil.
2. Arrange the bell pepper halves onto the prepared baking sheet, skin sides up and then with your hand, flatten each half.
3. Cook under the broiler for about 12 minutes.
4. Remove the bell pepper halves from the oven and immediately, transfer into a zip-top plastic bag.
5. Immediately, seal the bag and keep aside for about 10 minutes.
6. Peel the bell pepper halves and then, cut into 16 equal sized strips.
7. In a large bowl, dissolve the sugar and yeast in 1/2 C. of the warm water.
8. Keep aside for at least 5 minutes.
9. In the bowl of the yeast mixture, add the flour, salt and remaining 1/2 C of the water and mix until dough is formed.
10. Place the dough onto a floured surface and with your hands, knead until smooth.
11. Place the dough in a large greased bowl and turn to coat well.
12. Cover the bowl and keep aside in a warm place for at least 1 hour.
13. Now, set your oven to 450 degrees F and sprinkle a greased jellyroll pan with the

cornmeal.

14. Place the dough onto a floured surface and roll into a rectangle.
15. Arrange the dough rectangle onto the prepared baking sheet.
16. For the black bean spread: in a blender, add all the ingredients and pulse until smooth
17. Place about 1 1/2 C. of the black bean spread over dough rectangle evenly and top with the cheese.
18. Cook in the oven for about 13 minutes.
19. Remove from the oven and keep aside to cool for about 10 minutes.
20.   Meanwhile, for the chimichurri: in a bowl, add all the ingredients and mix well
21. Spread the chimichurri on top of the cheese evenly.
22. Cut the bread into 16 equal sized squares and serve with a topping of the bell pepper strips.

Chimichurri
Breakfast Frittata

Prep Time: 1 mins
Total Time: 4 mins

Servings per Recipe: 1
Calories	181.3
Fat	13.8g
Cholesterol	433.3mg
Sodium	167.0mg
Carbohydrates	0.7g
Protein	12.6g

Ingredients

2 large eggs
1 tbsp prepared chimichurri sauce

1 dash cream
1 tsp butter

Directions

1. In a bowl, add all the ingredients except the butter and mix until well combined.
2. In a frying pan, melt the butter over medium heat and cook the egg mixture for about 1 minute per side.
3. Serve hot.

BURGERS
Santa Domingo II

Prep Time: 10 mins
Total Time: 20 mins

Servings per Recipe: 1
Calories	441.6
Fat	22.7g
Cholesterol	66.9mg
Sodium	760.4mg
Carbohydrates	39.4g
Protein	20.2g

Ingredients
1 (10 oz.) packages angel hair coleslaw mix
1 lb. beef ground round, crumbled
1 large egg, lightly beaten
1/4 C. chopped cilantro
1/4 C. finely chopped onion
1 tsp chili powder
1 tsp ground cumin
1 tsp seasoning salt

2 tsp lime juice
1/4 C. ketchup
1/4 C. mayonnaise
12 dinner rolls, split
1 avocado, pitted, peeled and sliced
12 slices tomatoes
1 (14 oz.) round Chihuahua queso Blanco cheese, sliced

Directions
1. Set your grill for medium-high heat and lightly, grease the grill grate.
2. In a large pan, add the water over medium-high heat and bring to a boil.
3. Stir in the cabbage and immediately remove from the heat.
4. Keep the pan aside for about 5 minutes.
5. Drain the cabbage well and keep aside.
6. In a large bowl, add the beef, onion, cilantro, egg, lime juice, cumin, chili powder and seasoned salt and mix until well combined.
7. Make 12 equal sized small patties from the beef mixture.
8. Cook the patties onto the grill, covered for about 2-3 minutes per side.
9. Meanwhile, in a small bowl, add the mayonnaise and ketchup and mix until well combined
10. Spread the ketchup mixture over the cut sides of each roll evenly.
11. Arrange the hot burgers onto the bottom half of each roll, followed by the cheese, avocado, tomato and cabbage.
12. Cover with top half of the roll and serve.

Isabelle's Chimichurri Meatball Sandwiches

🥣 Prep Time: 30 mins
🕐 Total Time: 2 hr 30 mins

Servings per Recipe: 6
Calories	800.4
Fat	49.4g
Cholesterol	127.8mg
Sodium	1086.8mg
Carbohydrates	49.6g
Protein	37.8g

Ingredients

1 1/2 C. cilantro leaves, divided
1 C. parsley leaves, divided
6 garlic cloves, divided
1 1/2 lb. ground sirloin
1 C. soft breadcrumb
1/4 tsp dry crushed red pepper
1 large egg, lightly beaten
3/4 tsp kosher salt, divided
1/2 C. canola oil, divided
1/2 C. red wine vinegar

1 shallot, coarsely chopped
1 jalapeño pepper, coarsely chopped
2 tbsp oregano leaves
1/4 C. extra virgin olive oil
6 hoagie rolls, split
extra virgin olive oil
1 (10 oz.) packages shredded cabbage
1 C. crumbled Cotija cheese
lime wedge

Directions

1. Separate about 1/2 C. of the cilantro leaves and chop them.
2. Separate about 1/4 C. of the parsley leaves and chop them.
3. Separate 2 garlic cloves and mince them finely.
4. In a large bowl, add the chopped herbs and minced garlic.
5. In the bowl of the herbs, add the ground sirloin, breadcrumb, egg, red pepper and 1/4 tsp of the salt and gently, mix until well blended.
6. Make 18 equal sized balls from the meat mixture.
7. In a large nonstick skillet, heat 1 tbsp of the canola oil over medium-high heat and cook half of the meatballs for about 6 minutes, flipping occasionally.
8. In the bottom of a 6-quart slow cooker, place the cooked meatballs.
9. Repeat with 1 tbsp of the remaining canola oil and remaining meatballs.
10. In a food processor, add the vinegar, shallot, jalapeño pepper, oregano, remaining garlic, cilantro, parsley, canola oil and salt and pulse until well mixed.
11. In a bowl, add half of the herb mixture and 1/4 C. of the water and mix well.
12. Place the herb mixture over the meatballs evenly.
13. Set the slow cooker on Low and cook, covered for about 2 hours.

14. Meanwhile, set the broiler of your oven and arrange oven rack about 6-inch from the heating element.
15. With a slotted spoon, transfer the meatballs into a bowl, discarding mixture from the slow cooker.
16. In the bowl of the meatballs, add 1/4 C. of the reserved herb mixture and toss to coat well.
17. Coat the cut sides of each roll with the extra-virgin olive oil evenly.
18. Arrange the rolls onto a baking sheet and cook under the broiler for about 2 minutes.
19. In a bowl, add the shredded cabbage and 1/2 C. of the remaining herb mixture and toss to coat well.
20. Place the cabbage mixture onto each roll, followed by the meatballs and cheese.
21. Serve immediately alongside the remaining herb mixture and lime wedges.

Chicken
Gordon Chimichurri

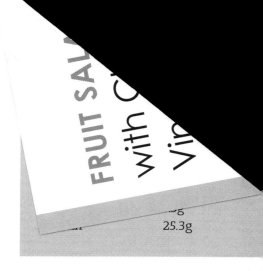

FRUIT SAL...
with C...
vi...

25.3g

Ingredients

6 boneless skinless chicken breasts
1 tsp ground pepper
1 1/2 tsp kosher salt
Sauce:
2 garlic cloves, minced
3 tbsp parsley, minced
1 tbsp minced cilantro
1 tbsp oregano
1 1/2 tsp kosher salt
ground black pepper

1 hot chili pepper
1 tsp red wine vinegar
2 tsp olive oil

Directions

1. Set your oven to 350 degrees F before doing anything else.
2. Arrange each chicken breast between 2 plastic wrap sheets and with a meat mallet, pound into a desired thickness.
3. Rub each chicken breast with the salt and pepper evenly.
4. For the chimichurri sauce: in a food processor, add the garlic, cilantro, parsley, oregano, Serrano, oil, vinegar, salt and black pepper and pulse until a smooth.
5. Spread about 1 tbsp of the sauce over each chicken fillet evenly.
6. Carefully, roll each breast around the sauce and then, secure with toothpicks.
7. Heat a greased grill pan and sear the rolled fillets for about 5 minutes.
8. Transfer the fillets onto a baking sheet and cook in the oven for about 15 minutes.
9. Serve hot.

...AD
...himichurri
...aigrette

Prep Time: 15 mins
Total Time: 25 mins

Servings per Recipe: 4
Calories	333.8
Fat	22.7g
Cholesterol	61.6mg
Sodium	611.0mg
Carbohydrates	15.2g
Protein	17.0g

Ingredients

8 oz. beef flank steak
1 tsp ground cumin
1/4 tsp salt
1 medium sweet onion, trimmed and sliced
2 tsp olive oil
1/4 tsp ground black pepper
6 C. Mache
4 ripe plums, pitted and cut into wedges

3/4 C. light mayonnaise
1/4 C. plain Greek yogurt
1 tbsp white vinegar
3 garlic cloves, minced
3 tbsp snipped Italian parsley
1/2 tsp crushed red pepper flakes
1/8 tsp salt

Directions

1. Set your gas grill for medium-high heat and lightly, grease the grill grate.
2. Season the steak with the salt and cumin evenly.
3. Coat the onion slices with the oil evenly and then, sprinkle with the pepper.
4. Arrange the steak and onion slices onto the grill rack directly over heat.
5. Cook the steak, covered for about 10 minutes, flipping once halfway through.
6. Cook the steak, covered for about 10-14 minutes, flipping once halfway through.
7. Remove the onion slices from the grill and place onto a platter.
8. Then, cut the onion slices roughly.
9. Remove the steak from the grill and place onto a cutting board for about 5 minutes.
10. Cut the steak into thin slices.
11. Meanwhile, for the chimichurri dressing: in a small bowl, add the garlic, yogurt, mayonnaise and vinegar and mix until well combined.
12. Stir in the parsley, red pepper and salt.
13. In a large serving bowl, mix together the steak, onion, plum and lettuce.
14. Serve immediately with a drizzling of the dressing.

Lunch Box
Pitas

Prep Time: 30 mins
Total Time: 45 mins

Servings per Recipe: 4	
Calories	440.5
Fat	18.1g
Cholesterol	51.0mg
Sodium	658.2mg
Carbohydrates	42.8g
Protein	26.0g

Ingredients

1/2 tsp ground coriander
1/2 tsp ground cumin
1/2 tsp salt
1/4 tsp pepper
12 oz. boneless beef sirloin, sliced and cut into strips
2 tbsp olive oil, divided
2 C. yellow onions, cut in thin lengthwise
24 inches pita bread rounds
1/2 C. chimichurri sauce
Sauce:

2 C. loosely packed flat leaf parsley, and tender stems
1/4 C. coarsely chopped onion
2 tbsp extra-virgin olive oil
1/4 C. red wine vinegar
1 tbsp oregano leaves
4 garlic cloves
1/2 tsp cayenne pepper
1 pinch sugar
salt and pepper

Directions

1. For the Chimichurri sauce: in a food processor, add all the ingredients and pulse until smooth.
2. In a large bowl, mix together the cumin, coriander, salt and pepper.
3. Add the sirloin strips and coat with the spice mixture slightly.
4. In a large skillet, heat 1 tbsp of the oil over medium-high heat and cook the onions for about 6 minutes, stirring occasionally.
5. In the same skillet, add the beef and remaining 1 tbsp of the oil and cook for about 3 minutes, stirring occasionally.
6. Remove from the heat and keep the aside, covered.
7. Meanwhile, place the pitas onto a microwave-safe plate and with a paper towel, cover them.
8. Microwave on High for about 1 minute.
9. Cut each pita in half to form 2 pockets.
10. Fill each pocket with the beef mixture.
11. Place about 1 tbsp of the chimichurri sauce over each pocket and serve.

CALIFORNIA
Honey Chimichurri

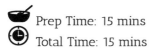 Prep Time: 15 mins

Total Time: 15 mins

Servings per Recipe: 1
Calories	1093.8
Fat	108.8g
Cholesterol	0.0mg
Sodium	1197.0mg
Carbohydrates	30.3g
Protein	3.1g

Ingredients
1/2 C. dried apricot
1 tsp honey
1 1/4 C. mint leaves
3/4 C. parsley, packed
1/2 C. cilantro, packed
2/3 C. red wine vinegar
4 garlic cloves, peeled
1 tsp kosher salt

1/2 tsp ground black pepper
1 tsp cumin
1 tsp lemon zest
1 pinch crushed red pepper flakes
1 - 1 1/4 C. extra virgin olive oil

Directions
1. In a bowl, add the honey, apricots and enough hot water to cover the apricots and keep aside for about 10 minutes.
2. Meanwhile, in a pan of the salted boiling water, add the parsley, cilantro and mint and boil for about 20 seconds.
3. Drain he herbs well and immediately, plunge in the ice bath.
4. Drain the herbs and the, spread onto a paper towel-lined baking sheet to dry.
5. Remove the apricots from the hot water and chop them roughly.
6. In a food processor, add all the ingredients except the olive oil and pulse until finely chopped.
7. While the motor is running, gradually add the oil and pulse until just combined.
8. Transfer the sauce into a bowl and refrigerate, covered for about 10 minutes.

Halibut
Griller

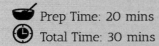
Prep Time: 20 mins
Total Time: 30 mins

Servings per Recipe: 4
Calories   401.3
Fat   10.2g
Cholesterol   190.8mg
Sodium   552.1mg
Carbohydrates   0.9g
Protein   71.8g

Ingredients

1 1/2 tbsp cilantro, chopped
1 tbsp basil, chopped
1 tbsp shallot, finely chopped
1 1/2 tbsp olive oil
1 1/2 tbsp lemon juice

1/2 tsp salt, divided
1/4 tsp black pepper, divided
cooking spray
4 halibut fillets

Directions

1. In a bowl, add the shallots, basil, cilantro, lemon juice, oil, 1/4 tsp of the salt and 1/8 tsp of the pepper and mix until well blended.
2. Season the halibut fillets with the remaining salt and pepper evenly.
3. Grease a grill pan with the cooking spray and heat over medium-high heat.
4. Add the halibut fillets and cook for about 4 minutes per side.
5. Place the chimichurri sauce over the halibut fillets and serve.

CHICKEN
Cutlets Chimichurri

Prep Time: 4 hr
Total Time: 4 hr 15 mins

Servings per Recipe: 4

Calories	1007.7
Fat	82.0g
Cholesterol	100.4mg
Sodium	1065.2mg
Carbohydrates	31.4g
Protein	38.5g

Ingredients

4 large boneless skinless chicken breast halves
1 C. prepared chimichurri sauce
2 tbsp canola oil
1 medium red onion, peeled and cut into strips
salt and pepper
4 sandwich buns, split
nonstick cooking spray
4 slices Monterey Jack cheese
1 ripe avocado, sliced

1 C. lettuce leaf
Sauce:
2 C. loosely packed flat leaf parsley sprigs
1/2 C. loosely packed cilantro stem
1 Serrano Chile, coarsely chopped
2 tbsp red wine vinegar
1 tbsp minced garlic
1 1/4 tsp kosher salt
1/4 tsp pepper
1 C. olive oil

Directions

1. For the chimichurri sauce: in a food processor, add the garlic, cilantro, parsley, Chile, vinegar, salt and pepper and pulse until finely chopped.

2. While the motor is running, slowly add the oil and 1 tbsp of water and pulse until smooth nicely.

3. For the chimichurri sandwiches: in a large zip lock bag, place the chicken and 3/4 C. of the chimichurri sauce.

4. Seal the bag and shake to coat well.

5. Refrigerate to marinate overnight.

6. Set your grill for medium-high heat and lightly, grease the grill grate.

7. Remove the chicken from bag and discard the marinade.

8. Cook the chicken onto the grill for about 2-4 minutes per side.

9. In the last minute of the cooking, place 1 cheese slice on top of each breast.

10. Remove the chicken from the grill and keep aside for about 5 minutes.

11. In a large skillet, heat the canola oil over medium heat and sauté the onion for about 8-10 minutes.

12. Stir in the salt and pepper and remove from the heat.
13. Place the remaining chimichurri sauce onto the cut side of each bun evenly.
14. Top each bun with a chicken breast, followed by the onions, avocado and lettuce.
15. Cover each with top bun and serve.

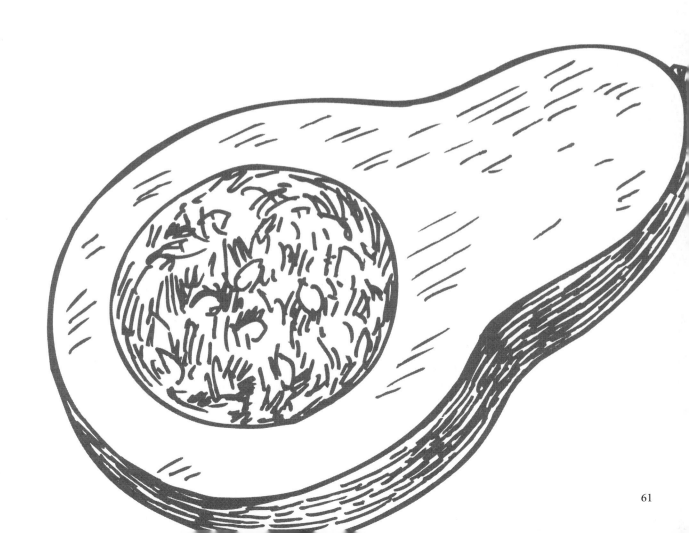

HOW TO MAKE
a Flank Steak

Prep Time: 10 mins
Total Time: 25 mins

Servings per Recipe: 8
Calories	222.1
Fat	12.8g
Cholesterol	77.1mg
Sodium	354.5mg
Carbohydrates	1.1g
Protein	24.3g

Ingredients
Sauce:
1/2 C. flat leaf parsley, packed
2 tbsp lemon juice
1/2 tsp crushed red pepper flakes
1/4 tsp kosher salt
1/4 tsp sugar
1/4 tsp cumin
1 large garlic clove

2 tbsp extra virgin olive oil
1 tbsp water
Meat:
2 lb. flank steaks, trimmed
3/4 tsp kosher salt
1/2 tsp black pepper, freshly ground
2 garlic cloves, minced
cooking spray

Directions
1. Set your grill for medium-high heat and lightly, grease the grill grate.
2. For the chimichurri sauce: in a food processor, add the garlic, parsley, lemon juice, sugar, cumin, red pepper flakes and salt and pulse until minced finely.
3. While the motor is running, slowly add the oil and 1 tbsp of water and pulse until well combined.
4. Rub the steak with the garlic clove evenly and then, sprinkle with the salt and pepper generously.
5. Place the steak onto the grill and cook, covered for about 6 minutes.
6. Flip and cook, covered for about 4 minutes.
7. Transfer the steak onto a cutting board and cover with a piece of foil for about 5 minutes.
8. Cut the steak into thin slices diagonally across the grain.
9. Serve the steak slices alongside the Chimichurri sauce.

Chimichurri
Zucchini and Squash with Potatoes

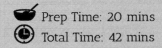

Prep Time: 20 mins
Total Time: 42 mins

Servings per Recipe: 4

Calories	687.1
Fat	19.7g
Cholesterol	0.0mg
Sodium	440.2mg
Carbohydrates	117.6g
Protein	16.0g

Ingredients
16 small red potatoes
1/3 C. olive oil
1/4 C. red wine vinegar
1/2 tsp salt
3 garlic cloves, minced
1 C. parsley, chopped
1/4 C. cilantro, chopped

2 medium zucchini, sliced
2 medium yellow squash, sliced
1 small red onion, trimmed, peeled, and cut into wedges

Directions
1. In a deep skillet, add the potatoes and enough water to cover over medium-high heat and bring to a boil.
2. Reduce the heat to a medium-low and simmer for about 10 minutes.
3. Drain the potatoes well and then, rinse them under cold running water.
4. Add the vinegar, oil and salt in a bowl and beat until blended nicely.
5. Add the garlic, cilantro and parsley and mix well.
6. In a zip lock bag, place the vegetables and 3/4 of the chimichurri sauce.
7. Seal the bag and shake to coat well.
8. Refrigerate to marinate for about 30-60 minutes.
9. Set your grill for medium-high heat and lightly, grease the grill grate.
10. Thread the vegetables onto 8 (10-inch) metal skewers alternately.
11. Cook the skewers onto the grill for about 6 minutes per side.
12. Serve the skewers alongside the remaining chimichurri sauce.

SONOMA
Black Bean Tacos

Prep Time: 30 mins
Total Time: 1 hr 15 mins

Servings per Recipe: 4

Calories	764.7
Fat	46.3g
Cholesterol	0.0mg
Sodium	1249.8mg
Carbohydrates	74.6g
Protein	15.9g

Ingredients

Brown Rice:
2 tbsp olive oil
1 onion, finely chopped
1/2 tsp sea salt
1 tomatoes, finely chopped
1/2 C. brown rice
1 C. vegetable broth
Sauce:
1 C. cilantro
1/2 C. Italian parsley
1/2 C. olive oil
1/4 C. lime juice
4 garlic cloves
2 tbsp agave syrup
1/2 tsp ground cumin

1 tsp sea salt
1/2 tsp ground black pepper
Filling:
2 tbsp olive oil
8 oz. cremini mushrooms, trimmed and sliced
1 (15 oz.) cans black beans, rinsed and drained
1 (8 oz.) packages flour tortillas
Finishing's:
sour cream
chopped tomato
sliced onion
shredded lettuce
diced avocado

Directions

1. For the tomato rice: heat the oil in a medium pan over medium-high heat and sauté the onions with the salt until tender.
2. Stir in the rice, tomato and broth and bring to a rolling boil over high heat.
3. Immediately, reduce the heat to low.
4. Cover the pan and simmer until all the liquid absorbs.
5. Remove from the heat and keep aside, covered for about 15 minutes.
6. For the chimichurri sauce: in a food processor, add the garlic, parsley, cilantro, agave nectar, lime juice, oil, cumin, salt and pepper and pulse until well blended.
7. In a small bowl, reserve half of the chimichurri sauce and keep aside.
8. For the filling: heat the oil in a large skillet over medium-high heat and cook the mushrooms for about 3-4 minutes.
9. Stir in the remaining chimichurri sauce and black beans and cook until heated completely.
10. Place the tomato rice in each tortilla, followed by the mushroom mixture, reserved chimichurri sauce, your favorite topping and sour cream.
11. Fold each tortilla like a burrito and serve.

Sopa de Papas
con Chimichurri

🥣 Prep Time: 10 mins
🕐 Total Time: 55 mins

Servings per Recipe: 6
Calories   132.6
Fat   9.1g
Cholesterol   32.0mg
Sodium   86.9mg
Carbohydrates   7.8g
Protein   5.2g

Ingredients

2 stalks celery & leaves
2 tbsp prepared chimichurri sauce
1 (20 oz.) packages Simply Potatoes Diced Potatoes with Onion

3 C. milk
1 C. half-and-half

Directions

1. Cut the celery stalk into 1/4-inch slices and then, mince the celery leaves finely.
2. Add the sandwich spread in a large, heavy pan over medium heat and cook until heated through.
3. Stir in the celery and celery leaves and cook until celery becomes crisp-tender.
4. Add the potato package and stir to combine.
5. Reduce the heat to medium-low and simmer for about 5 minutes, stirring frequently.
6. Stir in the half-and half and milk and simmer, covered for bout 20-30 minutes or until desired doneness.
7. Remove from the heat and serve immediately.

BURGERS
Argentino

Prep Time: 20 mins
Total Time: 30 mins

Servings per Recipe: 4
Calories	888.0
Fat	62.9g
Cholesterol	148.1mg
Sodium	808.0mg
Carbohydrates	32.7g
Protein	44.9g

Ingredients
Sauce:
2 garlic cloves, peeled
1 jalapeño pepper, stemmed, halved and seeded
3/4 C. packed stemmed parsley leaves
1/2 C. olive oil
2 tbsp red wine
1/4 tsp salt
1 1/2 tsp dried oregano leaves

1/2 tsp dried red pepper flakes
Patties:
1 1/2 lb. lean ground beef
salt
fresh ground black pepper
4 oz. Gouda cheese, cubes
4 Kaiser rolls, split

Directions
1. For the chimichurri sauce: in a food processor, add the jalapeño chile and garlic and pulse until finely minced.
2. Add the parsley and pulse until finely minced.
3. Add the vinegar, oil and salt and pulse until well blended.
4. In a small bowl, add the sauce mixture and stir in the oregano and red pepper flakes.
5. Keep aside for about 2 hours before using.
6. For the burgers: set your barbecue grill for medium-high heat and lightly, grease the grill grate.
7. In a large bowl, add the ground beef, 3 tbsp of the chimichurri sauce, salt and pepper and mix until well combined.
8. Make 8 (5-inch) equal sized patties from the mixture.
9. Place the cheese over 4 patties evenly.
10. Cover with the remaining patties and press the edges to seal the cheese.
11. Cook the patties onto the grill for about 5 minutes per side.
12. In the last 1 minute of cooking, place the buns onto the grill, cut sides down.
13. Place 1 patty in each bun and serve alongside the remaining chimichurri sauce.

Chimichurri
Chicago Steak House

Prep Time: 10 mins
Total Time: 10 mins

Servings per Recipe: 6
Calories	7.9
Fat	0.0g
Cholesterol	0.0mg
Sodium	52.0mg
Carbohydrates	1.7g
Protein	0.3g

Ingredients
1 green bell pepper, stemmed seeded and quartered
2 mild chiles, stemmed seeded and quartered
1 jalapeño pepper, halved
1/4 C. parsley

2 garlic cloves
3 tbsp pepperoncini peppers, chopped
3 tbsp red wine vinegar
salt

Directions
1. In a food processor, add the bell pepper, jalapeño pepper and mild chilies and pulse until finely chopped.
2. Add the remaining ingredients and pulse until slightly smooth.

SOUTH AMERICAN
Beef Kebabs

Prep Time: 4 hr
Total Time: 4 hr 8 mins

Servings per Recipe: 4
Calories	594.6
Fat	49.0g
Cholesterol	127.5mg
Sodium	530.8mg
Carbohydrates	2.8g
Protein	35.0g

Ingredients
1/3 C. lemon juice
3 C. cilantro, packed
3 garlic cloves
1 tsp crushed red pepper flakes
1 tsp dried oregano
1 tsp kosher salt

1/2 C. vegetable oil
1 1/2 lb. sirloin steaks, cut into cubes
8 bamboo skewers, soaked in water for 30 minutes

Directions
1. In a blender, add the garlic, cilantro, oil, lemon juice, oregano, pepper flakes and salt and pulse until pureed.
2. In an airtight container, place about 2/3 C. of the sauce and reserve in the refrigerator.
3. In a zip lock bag, add the beef cubes and remaining sauce and seal the bag after squeezing out the excess air.
4. Shake the bag well to coat and refrigerator to marinate for at least 4 hours or overnight, shaking the bag occasionally.
5. Set your grill for medium-high heat and lightly, grease the grill grate.
6. Remove the beef cubes from the bag and discard the excess marinade.
7. Thread the beef cubes onto pre-soaked skewers, leaving a little space.
8. Season the beef cubes with the salt evenly.
9. Cook the skewers onto the grill for about 3-4 minutes per side.
10. Serve immediately alongside the reserved chimichurri sauce.

Chimichurri
Mediterranean

🥣 Prep Time: 10 mins
🕐 Total Time: 10 mins

Servings per Recipe: 10
Calories	207.7
Fat	21.8g
Cholesterol	0.0mg
Sodium	182.5mg
Carbohydrates	4.2g
Protein	0.7g

Ingredients

8 garlic cloves, minced
1 tsp kosher salt
1 tsp oregano, dry leaves
1 tsp black pepper, ground
1 tsp red pepper flakes

3 lemons, zest
4 oz. lemon juice
1 bunch flat leaf parsley
1 C. olive oil

Directions

1. In a food processor, add all the ingredients and pulse until just combined.
2. Keep aside for about 30 minutes before serving.

FLANK
Steak del Barrio

Prep Time: 15 mins
Total Time: 35 mins

Servings per Recipe: 4
Calories	245.8
Fat	12.9g
Cholesterol	77.1mg
Sodium	502.6mg
Carbohydrates	6.5g
Protein	25.2g

Ingredients
1 tbsp olive oil
1/2 C. shallot, finely chopped
8 garlic cloves, minced
2 tbsp lemon juice
1 tbsp sherry wine vinegar
1/4 tsp crushed red pepper flakes
1 C. arugula, chopped
1/4 C. basil, finely chopped
1 tsp dried marjoram

3/4 tsp salt, divided
1/2 tsp pepper, divided
1/2 tsp smoked paprika
1 lb. flank steak
cooking spray

Directions
1. In a small nonstick skillet, heat the oil over medium-high heat and sauté the shallots and garlic for about 3 minutes.
2. Remove from the heat and stir in the vinegar, lemon juice and red pepper.
3. Keep aside to cool completely.
4. Set your grill for medium-high heat and lightly, grease the grill grate.
5. In a bowl, add the arugula, shallot mixture, marjoram, basil, 1/4 tsp of the salt and 1/4 tsp of the pepper and mix until well combined.
6. In a small bowl, mix together the paprika, remaining salt and pepper.
7. Rub the steak with the spice mixture evenly.
8. Cook the steak onto the grill for about 6 minutes per side.
9. Place the steak onto a cutting board for about 5 minute before slicing.
10. Cut the steak into thin slices diagonally across the grain.
11. Serve the steak slices with a topping of the sauce.

Argentinian x Mexico Bake

Prep Time: 15 mins
Total Time: 40 mins

Servings per Recipe: 8	
Calories	442.8
Fat	19.8g
Cholesterol	64.5mg
Sodium	811.5mg
Carbohydrates	44.0g
Protein	24.9g

Ingredients

1 (1 1/2 oz.) packets chimichurri seasoning
1 1/2 C. water
2 (8 oz.) cans tomato sauce
1 lb. ground beef
1 (15 oz.) cans black beans, rinsed and drained
1 (15 oz.) cans corn, drained
8 (8-inch) flour tortillas, warmed
1 1/2 C. Mexican blend cheese, shredded

Directions

1. Set your oven to 350 degrees F before doing anything else and lightly, grease a 13x9-inch baking dish.
2. In a bowl, add the tomato sauce, seasoning mix and water and mix until combined nicely.
3. Heat a large skillet over medium-high heat and cook the beef until browned completely.
4. Drain the grease from the skillet.
5. Remove from the heat and stir in the beans, corn and 1 C. of the sauce mixture.
6. Place about 1/2 C. of the beef mixture into each tortilla and carefully, fold like a burrito.
7. Arrange the burritos into the prepared baking dish, seam side down.
8. Spread the remaining sauce on top evenly, followed by the cheese.
9. Cook in the oven for about 15 minutes.

CHIMICHURRI
Aioli Glazed Tilapia

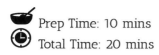

Prep Time: 10 mins
Total Time: 20 mins

Servings per Recipe: 8
Calories	7.9
Fat	0.0g
Cholesterol	0.0mg
Sodium	4.6mg
Carbohydrates	1.7g
Protein	0.3g

Ingredients

1/3 C. low-fat mayonnaise
2 tbsp lemon juice
1/3 C. diced onion
1 C. parsley
2 tbsp oregano

2 garlic cloves
8 tilapia fillets
2 tbsp Grated Parmesan Cheese

Directions

1. Set your grill for medium heat and lightly, grease the grill grate.
2. In a blender, add all the ingredients except the fish and cheese and pulse until well combined.
3. In a bowl, add half of the mayo mixture and reserve it.
4. Coat the tilapia fillets with the remaining mayo mixture evenly.
5. Cook the tilapia fillets onto the grill for about 3 minutes per side.
6. remove from the grill and immediately, top each fillet with the cheese.
7. Serve the tilapia fillets alongside the reserved mayo mixture.

Chimichurri
Lettuce Appetizers

🥣 Prep Time: 20 mins
🕐 Total Time: 20 mins

Servings per Recipe: 8
Calories	72.9
Fat	4.1g
Cholesterol	0.0mg
Sodium	21.0mg
Carbohydrates	8.3g
Protein	3.0g

Ingredients

2 tbsp extra virgin olive oil
1 tbsp red wine vinegar
1 minced garlic clove
1 fresh jalapeño chili
2 tbsp oregano leaves

1/2 C. flat leaf parsley
8 - 12 oz. queso fresco
3 romaine lettuce hearts

Directions

1. In a bowl, add all the ingredients except the queso fresco and lettuce and mix until well combined.
2. Fold in the queso fresco.
3. Arrange the romaine leaves onto a platter.
4. Place the sauce onto each leaf and serve.

CHIPOTLE
Parsley Halibut

Prep Time: 1 hr
Total Time: 1 hr 4 mins

Servings per Recipe: 6
Calories	278.8
Fat	11.8g
Cholesterol	102.8mg
Sodium	150.5mg
Carbohydrates	2.0g
Protein	39.0g

Ingredients
(6-oz) halibut fillets
1/4 C. shallot, diced
2 garlic cloves, minced
1 tbsp white wine vinegar
1 tbsp lemon juice, fresh
1 sprig thyme leave, chopped

1 sprig oregano, chopped finely
1/4 C. flat leaf parsley, fresh, chopped
1 tsp dried chipotle powder
1/4 C. extra virgin olive oil
salt and pepper

Directions
1. In a large bowl, add the shallots, garlic, lemon juice and vinegar and mix until well combined.
2. Keep aside for about 30 minutes before using.
3. In the bowl of the shallot mixture, add the herbs and mix until well combined.
4. Add the oil and chipotle and ix until well combined.
5. Add the halibut fillets and coat with the sauce generously.
6. Refrigerate to marinate for at least 30 minutes.
7. Remove the halibut fillets from the bowl and discard the marinade.
8. Set your grill and lightly, grease the grill grate.
9. Cook the halibut fillets onto the grill for about 2-3 minutes on each side.

Chimichurri
Tilapia

Prep Time: 10 mins
Total Time: 35 mins

Servings per Recipe: 4
Calories	147.9
Fat	15.5g
Cholesterol	5.0mg
Sodium	238.9mg
Carbohydrates	5.0g
Protein	0.8g

Ingredients

2 whole tilapia fish
aluminum foil
1 lemon, sliced
2 tsp seafood seasoning
2 tsp butter
1/4 C. flat-leaf Italian parsley, chopped

2 cloves, garlic, minced
1/2 tsp kosher salt
1/2 lemon, juiced
1/4 C. olive oil, extra virgin

Directions

1. Set your grill for medium-high heat.
2. Arrange each tilapia fish onto a greased square piece of foil.
3. Sprinkle the cavity and sides of each tilapia with the seafood seasoning evenly.
4. Arrange the lemon slices in the cavity of each tilapia and place the butter in the shape of dots.
5. Seal the foil around each fish to make a parcel.
6. Cook the parcels onto the grill for about 25 minutes.
7. For the sauce: in a small bowl, add the garlic, parsley, garlic, lemon juice, oil and mix until well combined.
8. Serve the fish alongside the sauce.

CATFISH
Córdoba

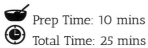 Prep Time: 10 mins

Total Time: 25 mins

Servings per Recipe: 4

Calories	362.8
Fat	26.5g
Cholesterol	79.8mg
Sodium	531.8mg
Carbohydrates	3.0g
Protein	27.0g

Ingredients
1/2 C. parsley
1/2 C. basil
1/4 C. cilantro
1/4 C. olive oil
1 garlic clove, minced
1 tbsp red wine vinegar
2 tsp lime juice
1/4 tsp ground cumin
3/4 tsp salt, divided

1/4 tsp ground pepper
1 1/2 lb. catfish fillets
1/4 C. orange juice
1/2 tsp orange zest

Directions
1. Set your oven to 425 degrees F before doing anything else and lightly, grease a baking dish.
2. Sprinkle the catfish fillets with the orange zest, 1/2 tsp of the salt ad 1/8 tsp of the pepper.
3. Arrange the catfish fillets into the prepared baking dish in a single layer and top with the orange juice evenly.
4. Cook in the oven for about 12 minutes.
5. Meanwhile, for the sauce: in a blender, add the garlic, cilantro, basil, parsley, vinegar, olive oil, lime juice, cumin, 1/4 tsp salt, 1/8 tsp pepper and pulse until smooth.
6. Serve the catfish alongside the sauce.

Cinnamon Cayenne
Rib Eye Clásico

🥣 Prep Time: 20 mins
🕐 Total Time: 15 mins

Servings per Recipe: 4
Calories	839.9
Fat	74.9g
Cholesterol	134.9mg
Sodium	567.5mg
Carbohydrates	5.3g
Protein	36.2g

Ingredients

1 tsp smoked paprika
1 tsp cumin
1 tsp coriander seed
1/2 tsp garlic powder
1/2 tsp cayenne pepper
1/2 tsp cinnamon
1/2 tsp sea salt
1/2 tsp black pepper
1 tbsp canola oil
2 (14 oz.) rib eye steaks
2 C. Italian parsley

1/2 C. picked mint leaf, no stems
1/2 C. extra virgin olive oil
3 garlic cloves
2 tbsp lemon juice
1 pinch sea salt

Directions

1. With a mortar and pestle, grind the coriander seeds, cumin, paprika, garlic powder, cayenne pepper, cinnamon, salt and black until coriander seeds are crushed and well combined.
2. Season the steaks with the spice mixture generously.
3. With a plastic wrap, cover the steaks and keep aside for about 20-30 minutes.
4. Meanwhile, for the sauce: in a food processor, add the garlic, mint, parsley, lemon juice, olive oil, 1 tsp of the spice mixture and salt and pulse until smooth.
5. Transfer the sauce into a container and refrigerate, covered until using.
6. Set your grill for medium-high heat with the lid closed and lightly, grease the grill grate.
7. Remove the plastic wrap from the steaks and coat them with the canola oil evenly.
8. Cook the steaks onto the grill for about 2 minutes.
9. Flip the steaks to 90 degrees and cook for about 2 minutes.
10. Flip and cook for about 2-3 minutes.
11. Place the steaks onto a cutting board for about 5 minutes before slicing.
12. Cut the steaks into desired slices and serve alongside the sauce.

ITALIAN
Tomato Chimichurri

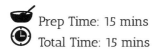 Prep Time: 15 mins
Total Time: 15 mins

Servings per Recipe: 6
Calories	179.9
Fat	18.2g
Cholesterol	0.0mg
Sodium	207.6mg
Carbohydrates	3.9g
Protein	1.0g

Ingredients
1/2 medium red onion, diced
1 bunch flat leaf parsley, chopped
2 Roma tomatoes, diced
5 garlic cloves, chopped
1/4 C. red wine vinegar
1/4 C. white vinegar

1/2 C. extra virgin olive oil
1/2 tsp salt
1/4 tsp black pepper
2 tbsp water

Directions
1. In a bowl, add all the ingredients and mix until well combined.
2. Refrigerate, covered for 2 hours tor up to overnight.

Orzo
Calabasas

Prep Time: 10 mins
Total Time: 35 mins

Servings per Recipe: 8

Calories	287.8
Fat	7.8g
Cholesterol	0.0mg
Sodium	297.9mg
Carbohydrates	46.1g
Protein	8.1g

Ingredients

4 garlic cloves, peeled
1/2 C. cilantro leaf
1/2 C. Italian flat leaf parsley
1/4 C. onion, chopped
1 poblano pepper, halved, seeded and chopped
2 tbsp lime juice
1 tsp salt

1/4 C. olive oil
fresh ground black pepper
1 (16 oz.) packages orzo pasta
1 red bell pepper, quartered, seeded and diced

Directions

1. In a food processor, with steel knife blade, add the onion, garlic, poblano, parsley, cilantro, lime juice and salt and pepper and pulse until pureed.
2. While the motor is running, slowly add the oil and pulse until well combined.
3. In a large pan, add the water and salt and bring to a boil.
4. Add the orzo and cook as directed by the package.
5. Drain the orzo well and transfer into a bowl.
6. Add the bell pepper and sauce and toss to coat well.
7. Serve immediately.

ARGENTINIAN
Oatmeal Fries

Prep Time: 5 mins
Total Time: 25 mins

Servings per Recipe: 1 batch	
Calories	201.3
Fat	18.6g
Cholesterol	3.6mg
Sodium	282.7mg
Carbohydrates	5.7g
Protein	4.1g

Ingredients
Fries:
6 tbsp white sesame seeds
1 C. cold cooked oatmeal
1/2 C. grated Parmigiano-Reggiano cheese
Sauce:
1 C. packed parsley leaves
1/4 C. packed cilantro leaves
2 garlic cloves, peeled
1/2 C. olive oil

1/3 C. red wine vinegar
3/4 tsp dried red pepper flakes
1/2 tsp ground cumin
1/2 tsp salt

Directions
1. Heat a dry frying pan over medium heat and cook the sesame seeds until toasted, shaking the pan occasionally.
2. Transfer the toasted sesame seeds onto a plate.
3. Make 8 equal sized balls from the oatmeal.
4. Coat each ball with the cheese and then roll into sesame seeds.
5. With your hands, flatten each ball slightly.
6. In a skillet, heat about 1/2-inch of vegetable oil over medium heat and cook the patties for about 10 minutes per side, pressing with the spatula slightly.
7. Remove from the heat and immediately, sprinkle with the sea salt slightly.
8. Meanwhile, for the sauce: in a food processor, add all the ingredients and pulse until smooth.
9. Serve the fritters with a topping of the sauce.

Chiang Mai x Houston
Chimichurri

Prep Time: 10 mins
Total Time: 10 mins

Servings per Recipe: 4
Calories	176.0
Fat	4.5g
Cholesterol	68.4mg
Sodium	455.1mg
Carbohydrates	4.5g
Protein	28.6g

Ingredients
3/4 C. bottled green chili salsa
1/4 C. unsweetened coconut milk
1 green onion, chopped
1/2 tsp shredded lime peel
1 tbsp lime juice
1 tbsp chopped cilantro
1 tbsp chopped of mint
1 tsp green curry paste
1 tsp grated ginger
1 tsp soy sauce
1 garlic clove, minced

4 boneless skinless chicken breast halves
chopped mango
chopped cucumber
mint

Directions
1. For the sauce: in a food processor, add the salsa, green onion, garlic, ginger, mint, cilantro, lime peel, coconut milk, lime juice, soy sauce and curry paste and pulse until smooth.
2. In a bowl, add 1/3 C. of the sauce and preserve in refrigerator until using.
3. In a large zip lock bag, place the chicken and remaining marinade.
4. Seal the bag and shake to coat well.
5. Refrigerate to marinate for about 1-2 hours, shaking the bag often.
6. Set your charcoal grill for medium heat and lightly, grease the grill grate.
7. Remove the chicken from the bag, reserving the marinade.
8. Place the chicken onto the grill directly over coals and cook for about 12-15 minutes, flipping once and coating with the reserved marinade halfway through.
9. Transfer the chicken onto a platter and drizzle with the reserved sauce.
10. Serve with a garnishing of the mint alongside the mango and cucumber.

GINGER
Honey Glazed Kebabs

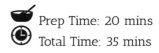 Prep Time: 20 mins

Total Time: 35 mins

Servings per Recipe: 16

Calories	167.0
Fat	16.0g
Cholesterol	17.2mg
Sodium	49.9mg
Carbohydrates	4.6g
Protein	1.6g

Ingredients

500 g beef, ground
1 onion
1/4 C. pine nuts, toasted
1 small hot pepper, deseeded and finely minced
3 garlic cloves, finely minced
1 slice bread, soaked in water, squeezed dry and crumbled
1 egg yolk
salt and pepper
1 tsp sweet paprika
1/4 tsp cumin
1/4 tsp baking soda
3 tbsp olive oil

Honey Glaze:
1/4 C. date honey
1/4 C. balsamic vinegar
1 tbsp ginger, finely minced
1 tbsp brown sugar
1/4 C. beef broth
salt and pepper
Sauce:
1 bunch parsley, coarsely minced
1/2 C. olive oil
1 small hot pepper, deseeded
1/4 C. white vinegar
3 - 5 garlic cloves
salt and pepper

Directions

1. For the kebabs: in a bowl, add the ground beef, onion, garlic, bread slice and pine nuts and mix until well combined.
2. In another bowl, add the olive oil, egg yolk, baking soda and spices and beat well.
3. Add the egg yolk mixture into the bowl of the beef mixture and with your hands, knead until well combined.
4. Keep aside for a few minutes.
5. With greased hands, make small balls from the beef mixture.
6. Shape each ball into kebab and freeze for a few minutes.
7. Set your oven to 450 degrees F and lightly, grease a baking sheet.
8. Arrange the kebabs onto the prepared baking sheet and cook in the oven for about 10 - 15 minutes.
9. For the ginger sauce: in a pan, add all the ingredients and bring to a boil.
10. Cook until the desired thickness of the sauce is achieved.
11. For the chimichurri: in a food processor, add all the ingredients except the oil and pulse until well combined.
12. While the motor is running, slowly add the oil and pulse until well combined.
13. Serve the kebabs alongside the both sauces.

Country
Sirloin Argentinian

Prep Time: 10 mins
Total Time: 26 mins

Servings per Recipe: 2
Calories	1192.2
Fat	78.4g
Cholesterol	333.2mg
Sodium	1130.1mg
Carbohydrates	13.8g
Protein	97.6g

Ingredients

1 1/2 lb. sirloin steaks, trimmed
1 1/2 C. cilantro stems
1 C. white vinegar
3/4 C. chopped onion
2 tsp ground cumin
2 tsp dried thyme
2 tsp cracked black pepper

1 tsp kosher salt
6 minced garlic cloves
3 bay leaves
cooking spray
chimichurri sauce

Directions

1. In a large re-sealable bag, add all the ingredients except the cooking spray and chimichurri sauce.
2. Seal the bag and shake well to coat completely.
3. Refrigerate to marinate for about 3 hours, shaking the bag occasionally.
4. Set your grill for medium heat and lightly, grease the grill grate.
5. Remove the steak from the bag and discard the marinade.
6. Cook the steak onto the grill for about 8 minutes per side.
7. Transfer the steak onto a cutting board for about 3 minutes before slicing.
8. With a sharp knife, cut the steak into thin slices diagonally across the grain.
9. Serve the steak slices alongside the chimichurri sauce.

CHIMICHURRI
Shrimp

Prep Time: 1 hr
Total Time: 1 hr 12 mins

Servings per Recipe: 6
Calories	481.5
Fat	35.9g
Cholesterol	98.7mg
Sodium	130.6mg
Carbohydrates	3.3g
Protein	35.4g

Ingredients
18 large shrimp
1 1/2 lb. skirt steaks
Sauce:
6 garlic cloves
2/3 C. olive oil
kosher salt & ground pepper

2 tbsp red wine vinegar
1 bunch flat leaf parsley, top leaves only
2 tbsp oregano leaves
1 lemon, juice

Directions
1. For the chimichurri sauce: in a food processor, add all the ingredients and pulse until smooth.
2. Transfer the chimichurri sauce into a large glass bowl.
3. Add the steak and shrimp and coat with the chimichurri sauce generously.
4. Refrigerate to marinate for about 1/2-1 hour.
5. Set your grill for high heat and lightly, grease the grill grate.
6. Place the steak onto the grill and cook for about 5 minutes.
7. Flip the steak and coat with some extra chimichurri sauce.
8. Coat the shrimp and coat with some extra chimichurri sauce.
9. Now, place the shrimp onto the grill with the steak and cook until desired doneness.
10. Transfer the steak and onto a platter.
11. With a sharp knife, cut the steak into thin slices diagonally across the grain.
12. Serve the steak and shrimp alongside the extra chimichurri sauce.

Chimichurri
Route-66

Prep Time: 5 mins
Total Time: 10 mins

Servings per Recipe: 10
Calories	97.1
Fat	10.8g
Cholesterol	0.0mg
Sodium	0.3mg
Carbohydrates	0.4g
Protein	0.0g

Ingredients

1 (27 oz.) cans tender green cactus pieces, in brine, drained
1/2 C. olive oil
1 garlic clove
1/2 lemon, juice

1/2 lime, juice
1 pinch red pepper flakes
salt & pepper
cilantro

Directions

1. In a food processor, add the cactus, garlic, cilantro, red pepper flakes, salt, pepper and juice of lime and lemon and pulse until chopped finely.
2. While the motor is running, slowly add the oil and pulse until well combined.

BURGERS
Brasileiro

Prep Time: 30 mins
Total Time: 48 mins

Servings per Recipe: 6

Calories	750.6
Fat	27.6g
Cholesterol	98.2mg
Sodium	717.4mg
Carbohydrates	90.9g
Protein	39.0g

Ingredients

1 tbsp ground cumin
1 C. cilantro leaves
1 C. Italian parsley
2 tbsp champagne vinegar
1 tsp crushed red pepper flakes
1/2 tsp coarse salt
1/4 C. canola oil
2 lb. lean ground beef

1/4 tsp salt
1/4 tsp ground red pepper
6 rolls, Mexican bolitos, split and toasted
1 tomatoes, sliced
1 onion, sliced
6 plantains, peeled and cut into slices

Directions

1. Set your grill for medium heat and lightly, grease the grill grate.
2. Heat a small frying pan over low heat and cook the cumin for about 2 minutes, stirring continuously.
3. Immediately, remove from the heat.
4. For the chimichurri sauce: in a blender, add the parsley, cilantro, vinegar, cumin, red pepper and salt and pulse on lowest speed until well combined.
5. While the motor is running, slowly add the oil and pulse until well combined.
6. In a large bowl, add the ground beef, 1/4 tsp of the salt and ground red pepper and mix until well combined.
7. Make (3 1/2-inch) 12 patties in from the beef mixture.
8. In the center of each of 6 patties, place 1 tbsp of the chimichurri sauce.
9. Cover each with the remaining patty and press the edges to seal the filling.
10. Arrange the patties onto the grill directly over the heat and cook for about 18-22 minutes, flipping once halfway through.
11. Transfer the patties onto a platter and cover with a piece of foil to keep warm.
12. Coat the plantain slices with the peanut oil evenly.
13. Arrange the plantain slices onto the grill directly over medium heat and cook for about 8 minutes, flipping once halfway through.
14. Remove from the grill and transfer the plantain slices onto a paper towel-lined plate to drain.
15. Spread a thin layer of the chimichurri sauce onto each roll and top with the burgers, followed by the remaining sauce, tomatoes and onions.
16. Serve the burgers alongside the plantain slices.

American-Mesa
Chimichurri

Prep Time: 15 mins
Total Time: 15 mins

Servings per Recipe: 4
Calories	168.9
Fat	18.1g
Cholesterol	0.0mg
Sodium	8.6mg
Carbohydrates	1.9g
Protein	0.6g

Ingredients

1/2 C. chopped cilantro
3/4 C. chopped Italian parsley
3 garlic cloves
1/2 C. red wine vinegar
1/3 C. olive oil
1 Serrano pepper

1/2 tsp cracked black pepper
1/2 tsp cumin
1 tsp season salt

Directions

1. In a food processor, add all the ingredients and pulse until smooth.

FISH
with Tropical Mango Chimichurri

Prep Time: 15 mins
Total Time: 25 mins

Servings per Recipe: 4
Calories	578.4
Fat	9.7g
Cholesterol	53.2mg
Sodium	266.4mg
Carbohydrates	79.3g
Protein	43.2g

Ingredients
1 C. mango
1/2 C. red bell pepper, seeded, ribs discarded, chopped
1/2 C. cilantro, chopped
1/2 C. parsley, chopped
1/4 C. lime juice
3 tbsp white wine vinegar
1 tbsp garlic, minced
1 tbsp dried oregano

2 tsp jalapeños, chopped
sea salt
ground black pepper
1 tbsp olive oil
1 lb. red snapper filets, cut into cubes, or white fish filets
1 (14 oz.) cans black beans, drained
1 C. cooked long grain brown rice, warm
4 flour tortillas

Directions
1. In a large bowl, add the mango, bell pepper, garlic, parsley, cilantro, jalapeño, vinegar, lime juice, oregano, 1/4 tsp of the salt and 1/4 tsp of the black pepper and mix well.
2. Season the snapper fillets with 1/4 tsp of the salt and 1/4 tsp of the black pepper.
3. In a large nonstick skillet, heat the oil over medium-high heat and cook the snapper fillets for about 5 minutes, flipping occasionally.
4. Stir in the rice and beans and cook for about 1-2 minutes.
5. Remove from the heat and stir in the mango mixture.
6. Place the snapper mixture onto each tortillas evenly.
7. Wrap each tortilla and serve.

6-Ingredient
Steak with Mock Chimichurri

Prep Time: 15 mins
Total Time: 1 hr 10 mins

Servings per Recipe: 8	
Calories	86.2
Fat	9.1g
Cholesterol	0.0mg
Sodium	8.9mg
Carbohydrates	1.1g
Protein	0.4g

Ingredients

1 C. A 1 garlic & herb marinade
2 C. parsley sprigs
1/3 C. olive oil

2 tbsp red wine vinegar
1 bay leaf
1 tsp dried oregano leaves

Directions

1. In a large bowl, add the steak and marinade and mix well.
2. Refrigerate for at least 30 minutes.
3. Set the broiler of your oven and arrange oven rack about 4-inch from the heating element. Grease a rack, arrange in a broiler pan.
4. Meanwhile, for the sauce: in a blender, add the remaining ingredients and pulse until smooth.
5. Transfer the sauce into a bowl and refrigerate before using.
6. Remove the steak from the bowl and discard the marinade.
7. Arrange the steak onto the prepared rack and cook under the broiler for about 5 minutes per side.
8. Transfer the steak onto a cutting board for about 5 minutes.
9. Cut the steak into thin slices diagonally across the grain.
10. Serve the steak slices alongside the sauce.

CHIMICHURRI
Havana

Prep Time: 20 mins
Total Time: 20 mins

Servings per Recipe: 8
Calories	89.3
Fat	9.0g
Cholesterol	0.0mg
Sodium	130.8mg
Carbohydrates	2.0g
Protein	0.6g

Ingredients
7 garlic cloves, peeled
1 1/4 C. packed cilantro leaves
3/4 C. packed parsley sprig
1 tsp crushed red pepper flakes
1 tsp coarse ground black pepper
1/4 C. white balsamic vinegar
2 tbsp lime juice

1 tbsp soy sauce
1/2 tsp lime zest
1/3 C. olive oil
grilled steak

Directions
1. In a small food processor, add the garlic, parsley, cilantro, pepper flakes and pepper and pulse until finely chopped.
2. Add the soy sauce, lime juice, vinegar and lime peel and pulse until well combined.
3. While the motor is running, slowly add the oil and pulse until well combined.
4. Serve the steak alongside the sauce.

Eliza's
Chimichurri

Prep Time: 10 mins
Total Time: 10 mins

Servings per Recipe: 1
Calories	1334.4
Fat	144.6g
Cholesterol	0.0mg
Sodium	2358.0mg
Carbohydrates	14.0g
Protein	2.6g

Ingredients

1 C. flat leaf parsley, chopped fine
1/2 C. cilantro, chopped fine
2 tbsp thyme, stemmed and chopped fine
1/2 C. white onion, minced
1 C. extra virgin olive oil
1 tbsp garlic, minced
2 tbsp lemon juice

1 tbsp lime juice
2 tsp kosher salt
1/2 tsp cumin
1 tsp ground black pepper

Directions

1. Add all the ingredients in a food processor and pulse until smooth.
2. Transfer the sauce into a bowl and refrigerate, covered for at least 1 hour or up to three days.

ROASTED
Peppermint Roast

Prep Time: 2 hrs
Total Time: 6 hrs

Servings per Recipe: 8
Calories	46.4
Fat	3.4g
Cholesterol	0.0mg
Sodium	0.8mg
Carbohydrates	4.3g
Protein	0.1g

Ingredients
2 - 3 lb. well-trimmed tri-tip roast
1/4 C. lime juice
2 tbsp olive oil
1/4 C. minced cilantro
1 tbsp minced green onion
2 garlic cloves, minced
1 tbsp minced peppermint

1/2 tbsp ground pepper
2 tbsp sugar
salt

Directions
1. In a large re-sealable bag, add the roast, green onion, garlic, mint, cilantro, oil and lime juice.
2. Seal the bag and shake to coat well.
3. Refrigerate for about 2 hours.
4. Set your smoker for an indirect temperature between 225 and 250°F.
5. Arrange the roast with the marinade in the center of a foil piece of foil.
6. Wrap the foil around the meat loosely to make a pouch.
7. Cook the wrapped meat in smoker for about 3 hours.
8. Remove the meat from the foil pouch and cook in the smoker for about 30 minutes, flipping once halfway through.
9. Transfer the meat onto a cutting board.
10. Cut the meat into desired sized pieces.
11. Carefully, place the foil juice into a skillet over medium heat.
12. Add the sugar and pepper and cook until the mixture reduced by half.
13. Stir in the meat pieces and remove from the heat.
14. Serve hot.

Picnic
Chimichurri

Prep Time: 7 hr
Total Time: 7 hr

Servings per Recipe: 1
Calories	2129.4
Fat	220.7g
Cholesterol	0.0mg
Sodium	7044.9mg
Carbohydrates	51.7g
Protein	9.5g

Ingredients
6 garlic cloves, peeled
1 C. packed flat-leaf parsley
1 C. packed cilantro
3 green onions
1/4 C. oregano leaves
1 jalapeño, stem removed
1 tbsp kosher salt
1 tbsp black pepper
1 tsp red pepper flakes
1 tbsp smoked paprika

1 C. extra virgin olive oil
1/2 C. red wine vinegar
1/4 C. water
2 limes, juiced

Directions
1. In a food processor, add all the ingredients and pulse until well combined.
2. In a 1 gallon re-sealable bag, place the meat and chimichurri and seal the bag after squeezing out the excess air.
3. Refrigerate for about 6-7 hours, shaking the bag often.
4. Remove the meat from the bowl and discard the marinade.
5. Keep the meat at the room temperature for about 20-30 minutes before cooking.
6. Cook the meat onto grill until cooked through.

BUENOS AIRES
Brisket

Prep Time: 45 mins
Total Time: 4 hr 15 mins

Servings per Recipe: 6
Calories   851.4
Fat   70.5g
Cholesterol   193.1mg
Sodium   180.6mg
Carbohydrates   3.4g
Protein   45.7g

Ingredients

Sauce:
7 garlic cloves, peeled
4 jalapeño peppers, seeded and chopped
7 bay leaves
1 1/4 C. flat leaf parsley
2/3 C. cilantro leaf
2 1/2 tbsp dried oregano

1 1/4 C. distilled white vinegar
kosher salt
2 C. water
Beef:
3 1/2 lb. beef brisket, soaked in cold water to cover for 1 hour, drained

Directions

1. For the chimichurri: in a food processor, add the jalapeños, garlic and bay leaves and pulse until chopped finely.
2. Add the cilantro, oregano and parsley and pulse until chopped finely.
3. While machine running, add the oil and vinegar and pulse until smooth.
4. Add the salt and pulse to combine.
5. Transfer 1 C. of the chimichurri into a container and refrigerate, covered until using.
6. In a large ceramic baking dish add the water and remaining chimichurri and mix until well combined.
7. Add the brisket and coat with the marinade generously.
8. With a plastic wrap, cover the baking dish and refrigerate for about 24-48 hours.
9. Set your oven to 350 degrees F and arrange a rack in the center of the oven.
10. In a roasting pan, place the brisket with marinade.
11. Cover the roasting pan and cook in the oven for about 3 1/2 hours.
12. Remove from the oven and place the brisket onto a cutting board to cool slightly before slicing.
13. Cut the brisket into desired sized slices diagonally.
14. Meanwhile, in a microwave-safe bowl, add the reserved chimichurri and microwave until heated slightingly.
15. Serve the brisket slices alongside the chimichurri sauce.

Red Pepper Rib-Eye with Balsamic Chimichurri

Prep Time: 15 mins
Total Time: 30 mins

Servings per Recipe: 4
Calories	135.9
Fat	12.5g
Cholesterol	15.2mg
Sodium	60.3mg
Carbohydrates	5.0g
Protein	0.3g

Ingredients

1/2 C. packed chopped cilantro
6 tbsp balsamic vinegar
2 tbsp olive oil
2 garlic cloves, peeled and minced
1 tsp adobo seasoning
1/2 tsp dried oregano
1/2 tsp pepper

1/4 tsp dried red chili pepper flakes
2 boned beef rib eye steaks
2 tsp steak herb seasoning mix
2 tbsp butter

Directions

1. For the chimichurri sauce: in a bowl, add the garlic, cilantro, oil, vinegar, oregano, adobo seasoning, pepper, and chile flakes and mix until well combined.
2. Rub each steak with the seasoning mix evenly.
3. In a 10-12-inch nonstick frying pan, melt 1 tsp of the butter over medium-high heat and cook the steaks for about 10 minutes, flipping frequently.
4. Place the steaks onto a platter and cover with a piece of foil to keep warm.
5. In the same pan, melt the remaining butter and stir in the chimichurri sauce.
6. Cut each steak into 2 equal sized pieces.
7. Arrange the steak pieces onto the serving plates.
8. Transfer any meat juices from the platter into the frying pan and combine it with the sauce.
9. Pour the sauce mixture over the steak pieces and serve.

MANHATTAN
Strip Steaks

Prep Time: 15 mins
Total Time: 30 mins

Servings per Recipe: 4
Calories	1271.2
Fat	106.7g
Cholesterol	275.5mg
Sodium	180.2mg
Carbohydrates	4.7g
Protein	70.7g

Ingredients
4 (12 oz.) New York strip steaks
salt & pepper
Sauce:
1 C. Spanish olive oil
2 limes, juice
4 garlic cloves
2 shallots, minced

1 tbsp basil, minced
1 tbsp thyme
1 tbsp oregano leaves
salt and pepper

Directions
1. For the chimichurri marinade: in a bowl, add all the ingredients and mix until well combined.
2. In a large baking dish, add the steaks and half of the chimichurri marinade mix well.
3. Refrigerate, covered for about 2 hours.
4. Set your grill for high heat and lightly, grease the grill grate.
5. Remove the steaks from the refrigerator and keep aside in room temperature for about 20 minutes before cooking.
6. Remove the steak from the bowl and discard the marinade.
7. Sprinkle each steak with the salt and pepper evenly.
8. Cook the steaks onto the grill for about 4-5 minutes per side.
9. Remove the steaks from the grill and place onto a platter for about 10 minutes before serving.
10. Serve the steaks alongside the remaining chimichurri sauce.

Rosario
Chimichurri

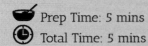 Prep Time: 5 mins

Total Time: 5 mins

Servings per Recipe: 1

Calories	1040.5
Fat	109.8g
Cholesterol	0.0mg
Sodium	3530.4mg
Carbohydrates	17.7g
Protein	4.1g

Ingredients

6 garlic cloves, minced
2 shallots, minced
2 C. parsley, minced
1/4 C. oregano leaves, minced
1 tbsp salt

1 tsp red pepper flakes
1 C. olive oil
1/2 C. red wine vinegar
1/4 C. water

Directions

1. In a bowl, add all the ingredients and with a whisk, mix until well combined.
2. Any kind of meat or veggies can be marinated in his sauce.

CUMIN
Coriander Flank Steak

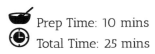

Prep Time: 10 mins
Total Time: 25 mins

Servings per Recipe: 4
Calories   456.8
Fat   32.4g
Cholesterol   115.6mg
Sodium   763.2mg
Carbohydrates   2.6g
Protein   37.0g

Ingredients
1 1/2 lb. flank steaks
Spice Mix:
1 1/2 tsp kosher salt
1/2 tsp ground coriander
1/2 tsp ground cumin
1/4 tsp black pepper
Sauce:

2 cloves garlic, minced
1 1/2 C. cilantro
1 1/2 C. flat leaf parsley
1/4 C. white vinegar
1/3 C. olive oil
1/4 tsp cayenne

Directions
1. Set the broiler of your oven and arrange oven rack about 4-inch from the heating element.
2. For the rub: in a bowl, add all the ingredients and mix well.
3. Rub the steak with the rub mixture generously.
4. Cook the steak under the broiler for about 6 minutes on both sides.
5. Meanwhile, for the chimichurri sauce: add all the ingredients in a food processor and pulse until finely chopped.
6. Remove the steak from the oven and place onto a cutting board for about 5 minutes.
7. With a sharp knife, cut the steak into thin slices diagonally.
8. Serve alongside the chimichurri sauce.

LEMON LIME
Skirt Steak with Chimichurri

 Prep Time: 2 hr 30 mins
Total Time: 2 hr 40 mins

Servings per Recipe: 4
Calories	488.6
Fat	30.8g
Cholesterol	100.3mg
Sodium	1007.2mg
Carbohydrates	4.9g
Protein	46.3g

Ingredients
Skirt:
1 tsp garlic, minced
1 tsp cilantro leaf, chopped
2 tbsp olive oil
3 tbsp tequila
1 tbsp lemon juice, squeezed
1 tbsp lime juice, freshly squeezed
1/2 tsp salt
1 tsp black pepper, cracked
1 1/2 lb. skirt steaks, trimmed
Sauce:
2 tbsp cilantro leaves, chopped
2 tbsp parsley leaves, chopped

1 tbsp basil leaves, chopped
1 tbsp oregano leaves, chopped
2 tbsp white onions, minced
2 tbsp red bell peppers, diced
2 tbsp garlic, minced
1 tsp salt
1 tbsp black pepper, cracked
1/2 tsp ground cumin
2 tbsp red wine vinegar
1 tbsp dried pasilla pepper
2 tbsp extra virgin olive oil

Directions
1. For the steak: in a large bowl, add all the steak and mix until well combined.
2. Add the steak and oat with the marinade generously.
3. Refrigerate to marinate for about 1-3 hours.
4. Meanwhile, for the chimichurri sauce: in a food processor, add all the ingredients and gently, stir to combine.
5. Transfer the sauce into a bowl and keep aside for about 2 hours before serving.
6. Set your grill for high heat and lightly, grease the grill grate.
7. Remove the steak from the bowl and discard the marinade.
8. Cook the steak onto the grill for about 5-10 minutes or until desired doneness.
9. Remove the steak from the grill and place onto a cutting board.
10. Cut the steak into 1/4-inch pieces against the grain.
11. Serve the steak pieces with a topping of the chimichurri sauce.

Printed in Great Britain
by Amazon